Africa is blessed with a rich diversity of cul[...]
However, such diversity can also lead to c[...]
religious outlook. The situation becomes much more complex when there are
unequal power relations, competition for limited material resources, and a history of conflict. Prof. Agang addresses concerns such as these with clarity and
wisdom as he draws upon the biblical motif of the "remnant." He rightly shows
that the loving power of God supersedes the powers of all political, cultural,
economic and ethnic identities. The key to peace and human flourishing, he
proposes, is a clearer understanding of the implications of living in a covenantal
relationship with God and all of God's creation. This book contains a wealth of
theological and pragmatic wisdom to aid "remnant" minority communities and
those who occupy majority social positions to live more justly and faithfully
for the sake of God's perfect will and the achievement of the common good.
This is a very important book!

Dion A. Forster, PhD
Director, Beyers Naudé Centre for Public Theology
Chair, Department of Systematic Theology and Ecclesiology,
University of Stellenbosch, South Africa

The first sentence of the preface to *God of the Remnant* grabbed me and I read
the book non-stop. Sunday Agang is familiar with the fate of minorities in
Africa. He knows suffering, but he found a door that unlocks a road less travelled. He explains what "remnant" means in Scripture and how God uses small
minorities through difficult times to keep faith and hope alive. In doing so,
Agang gives the reader a set of glasses – one can see the patterns of history! The
majesty of the covenantal God unfolds. Being in the presence of God changes
the way you see yourself: identity gets redefined, self-confidence is regained,
shame is removed, despair vanishes and hope is rekindled. The acceptance of
being a remnant is not an instant individualized cure from miseries leading
to a hassle-free life! In this book, you are invited to take the first steps on an
Abrahamic journey and before your very eyes the footprints of the one who
set aside the privileges of deity appear.

H. Jurgens Hendriks, DLitt
Emeritus Professor, Practical Theology and Missiology,
Stellenbosch University, South Africa
Program Coordinator, Network for African Congregational Theology (NetACT)

The task of the theologian is two-fold; namely, to understand the message of the Bible and to apply that message to the contemporary situation. In *God of the Remnant: The Plight of Minority Ethnic Groups in Africa*, Professor Sunday Agang has not only brought out the meaning of the biblical concept of remnant but applied it to the plight of many ethnic minorities. There are thousands of ethnic minority groups all over Africa who suffer all kinds of indignities such as isolation, oppression, intimidation, deprivation, poverty, violence and despair. Juxtapose the plight of ethnic minorities with the majority ethnic groups who live in affluence, protection, and prosperity and oppress minority groups. These extreme realities and tensions are with us and the Christian must make sense of it all.

Agang emphasizes that God is the one who gives *love, mercy, grace and hope* for those who are victims of violence and extreme social ills. This is an apt study that will find meaning and relevance for the many struggles, questions, tensions and severe afflictions of many African ethnic minorities.

Samuel Waje Kunhiyop, PhD
Professor of Systematic Theology and Ethics,
ECWA Theological Seminary, Kagoro, Nigeria
Author, *African Christian Ethics*

This book by Professor Sunday Agang speaks powerfully to the situation of the minority ethnic groups in Africa. *Marginalization* is the key word that describes their fate. Citing the example of Nigeria, the colonial masters empowered three regions: namely, North, East, and West. In these regions, the key players are the Hausa, Fulani, Igbo, and Yoruba. The rest of the over five hundred minority nationalities became subsumed non-entities and mere numbers to be manipulated for political gains by the majority tribes. These minority ethnic groups are despised, marginalized, persecuted, and downtrodden. But Prof. Agang does not stop in this state of hopelessness and despair. From the biblical concept of the remnant, he sees a "beacon of hope" for the minorities – they can serve as a source of blessing to the rest of humankind. What a huge encouragement for the marginalized and discouraged remnant! I enthusiastically recommend this book for the persecuted remnant in Africa and beyond.

Rev. Bitrus A. Sarma, PhD
Professor of Biblical Studies (NT),
Provost, ECWA Theological Seminary, Kagoro, Nigeria

God of the Remnant

HIPPOBOOKS

God of the Remnant

The Plight of Minority Ethnic Groups in Africa

Sunday Bobai Agang

Africa Christian Textbooks (ACTS), TCNN, PMB 2020, Bukuru 930008, Plateau State, Nigeria
www.actsnigeria.org

Langham Publishing, PO Box 296, Carlisle, Cumbria, CA3 9WZ, UK
www.langhampublishing.org

ISBNs:
978-1-83973-058-0 Print
978-1-83973-477-9 ePub
978-1-83973-478-6 Mobi
978-1-83973-479-3 PDF

British Library Cataloguing-in-Publication Data
A catalogue record for this book is available from the British Library

ISBN: 978-1-83973-058-0

Cover & Book Design: projectluz.com

Contents

Foreword

Sunday Agang has already shown himself repeatedly as a scholar committed to the practical needs of the church and society, an advocate for peace, justice and truth. In this eloquent and passionate book, he sounds a biblical call to heed the minorities in our midst.

He reminds us that this is a biblical pattern, and examples could be multiplied. In Genesis, God often chose the younger sibling, against conventional expectations (I recognize this as a biologically eldest sibling myself!). As in the case of Abraham, or his choice of Israel in Egypt, or the Hellenist ministers in Acts 6, God often chooses what is small as the promise of the future. (Those Hellenist Jews of Acts 6 became the initial bridge to the later Gentile majority church.) Jeremiah spoke as a tiny and despised remnant in his day, but the next generation recognized that he was the one true prophet of his generation. Whereas Caesar, who orders the census in Luke 2, was hailed as divine and reigned from a palace, a few verses later Jesus is born in a manger. He grew up in obscure Nazareth rather than in famed Jerusalem. His kingdom, that will one day rule the earth, first arrived on the scene like a tiny mustard seed, or a bit of yeast stirred into a loaf. In most generations, those faithful to God within Israel were a remnant, and Israel itself at its best was a tiny witness for a monotheism that now, in different ways, underlies the world's two largest religions.

God works through what is small, showing that he is not dependent on what mere humans think is big. He is near the lowly and the broken, but far from the proud, so we are most apt to encounter his presence among the lowly. Throughout history, initially persecuted groups have often emerged as leading voices for the church or at least offering major contributions to the church. In my own country, some ethnic and theological groups once socially marginalized now have an increasing prophetic voice for all the church. Such observations should remind us how God values minorities and remnants. The church as Christ's body can be whole only as we heed all the Spirit-directed voices among us. As Dr. Agang helps give voice to the remnant, may we heed that voice, whether we belong to majorities or minorities.

Craig Keener, PhD
Asbury Theological Seminary

Preface

I know from my own experience that life is not easy as a member of a minority group in Africa. Your options are limited and you and your people are at the mercy of majorities who control all aspects of community life. Sometimes, your group is made the scapegoat for problems in the community. You may even endure severe persecution. At best, you may hope to be ignored, and you have resigned yourself to "spare-tyre status" as a permanent second-class citizen.

But I have found another option, a beacon of hope lit by the biblical concept of remnant, that should change your perspective dramatically. I pray that as you study this book, you will be encouraged to see yourself and your people from God's perspective and to realize how much he values remnants and minorities. In his eyes, they are often the source of great blessings to humanity. May the pastors, teachers and students who read this book in violent conflict-ridden societies start to see themselves from this new perspective and have assurance of a future with hope.

Some who read this book may also be from majority groups. I pray that as you read you will recognize how insidious the effects of power can be and will examine your own thinking and your own life, so that you can be transformed into one who celebrates God's creation order of equality and wholesomeness.

Once you have read this book, you may want to know more about how you can act to further transform your own thinking and the society around you. To that end, I have added a list of further reading at the back of the book. I would particularly recommend that you read *African Public Theology*, a book that presents the ideas of scholars from across Africa on how we can reposition Africa to be the Africa God wants, an Africa that values human dignity far more than self-interest and power. My own studies in remnant theology, presented in this book, shaped my contribution to that volume, and reading it will enrich your understanding of the issues involved in this present volume.

Rev. Prof. Sunday Bobai Agang
Jos, Nigeria, 2021

Acknowledgements

Writing a book that takes many years of research and reflection makes one indebted to many people, too many to remember to say thank you to. Thus I will only attempt to acknowledge a few here. There are the many authors who contributed tremendously to my understanding of the subject matter, and the many mentors, financial supporters and colleagues who have given me the opportunities I needed to be able to get this work done. For example, I sincerely thank Mr Don Erwin, who was my BA thesis supervisor at ECWA Theological Seminary in Jos when I first researched the concept of the remnant in Paul's writings. I remain deeply indebted to Langham Partnership International and ScholarLeaders International for financial and moral support throughout my doctoral studies at Fuller. I sincerely thank my MDiv and PhD mentors, Prof. Ron Sider of Eastern Baptist Theological Seminary (now Palmer Theological Seminary, Philadelphia) and Professors Glen Stassen and Colin Brown of blessed memories at Fuller Theological Seminary, Pasadena, CA. They taught me how to pay careful attention to issues of love, justice, peace and compassion, and through their deep commitment to research and writing for the church and society they encouraged me to write for the benefit of the church and society, particularly in Africa.

I thank Professors Jurgens Hendriks and Dion Forster, both of Stellenbosch University, for granting me the opportunity to spend a sabbatical at the Beyers Naude Centre for Public Theology at Stellenbosch University in 2018. I thank Langham Partnership for approving a grant that enabled me to travel to South Africa and spend quality time doing this research. My gratitude also goes to the Board of Governors of ECWA Theological Seminary Kagoro (ETSK) for overwhelmingly approving my application for a sabbatical in 2018.

I am most grateful to God Almighty who has granted me good health as well as the ability to write this book on the God of Israel's remnant and Africa's vulnerable minorities. I specifically thank God for connecting me with a fine team of editors, Isobel Stevenson and Morag Venter. They demonstrated their profound love of the church by enthusiastically devoting their time to ensuring that this book would reach its readers. They did an excellent job of revising, editing and restructuring the chapters to make the entire book flow logically, cohesively, and clearly. I am profoundly grateful to them for a job well done.

Finally, I thank my wife, Sarah, and our children, Nancy, Esther, Kent and Dorcas, who stood by me in prayers and encouraged me to write this book for the benefit of the church and society in Africa.

1

Introduction

Why would anyone want to read a book on remnant theology? That is a very good question, and one that I myself would have asked if you had handed me this book when I was a young man. I wanted to read – and write – books that were relevant to the political, religious and economic crises of contemporary Africa. But over time, as I have grown in my knowledge of God, the Scriptures and Africa, I have come to see that remnant theology has enormous relevance to Africa.

Let me begin by telling you how I came to see this link. Then maybe you will be prepared to study it with me, and to live out what you learn incarnationally in Africa.

My interest in this topic began in the early 1990s when I wrote my BA thesis on Paul's concept of the remnant. At that time, I was trying to understand how Paul used the idea of a remnant to explain to the Jews how God had interacted with them throughout their history. My primary focus was on gaining a fuller grasp of the history of salvation. It was an academic topic, rather than one that deeply shaped my everyday life as a Nigerian.

What did shape my life as a Nigerian was the fact that I was born into a minority group. Nigeria has four major ethnic groups: the Hausa, Fulani, Yoruba, and Igbo. I belong to none of those groups, but I have watched the conflicts between them ever since the Biafran War first affected my life as a young boy. I heard rumours about what members of majority groups were doing to my people. For example, it was said that they were digging pits inside their homes so that woman from my group who entered their homes would fall into the pit and die there. Ludicrous as such rumours were, I learned to be afraid. As I matured into manhood, I watched how these rivalries played out around me. There was plenty of scope for observation.

As I did my graduate studies and contemplated the power struggles of competing majorities and the trampling of minority rights in Nigeria and elsewhere in Africa, I found my mind returning to the idea of the remnant. I began to wonder whether the concept of a remnant applied only to the Jewish nation in the past, or whether it still had relevance today. Could the remnant motif in Scripture have any impact in our society today? Would it have liberating implications for people living in very different contexts from those of the biblical authors? Could our knowledge of how God saw and used remnants in ancient times shape and transform our thinking so that we would no longer be tempted to passively accept or even actively uphold human hierarchies, whether social, political, spiritual or economic? Could the remnant motif infuse us with greater self-understanding and imagination so that we would become more self-aware? I was wrestling with the question of whether the biblical teaching about a remnant has practical implications for Africa today. Does it have profound implications for how we live in multi-ethnic societies, for how we see ourselves, and how we treat members of other ethnic groups?

I think it does. Although the term 'remnant' is not often used in Africa, we have groups which fall into this category, specifically our many ethnic minorities. In much of Africa ethnic majorities believe that their numbers and social status gives them the right to deprive ethnic minorities of their human rights, with the result that many Africans are unable to realize their God-given potential and use their gifts for the good of church and society. We as Christians need to reflect on our participation in this game of numbers. This book is an invitation to take stock, to dig deeper, and to think harder about what can be gleaned from remnant theology so that we can refocus our social, political, spiritual and economic life. If we do so, the implications of remnant theology could become part of the solution to the social, political, and moral crises that affect our continent so deeply.

In the chapters of this book, I share with you what I have learned as I have meditated on this topic and asked myself the questions asked above and invite you to follow the same path that I trod as I grew in insight. I begin by dealing with the places in the Bible where the remnant motif is explicitly mentioned. So we will consider the message of prophets like Isaiah, the experience of the remnant in the days of Ezra and Nehemiah, and the New Testament perspective of Paul.

Looking at these writings and what they have to say about the experiences of the remnant in their day will open our minds to think about who qualifies to be regarded as a remnant today. Which groups in Africa have had experiences similar to those of the people described in the Bible? How does what the Bible says apply to them? Does it apply at all? After all, the prophets were speaking to the Old Testament people of God, not to Africans today. Do we have any right to assume that the promises God gave to the Israelites apply to us?

That is a valid question, and deserves a solid answer. The clue to the correct answer, I believe, lies in the recognition that the Bible's teaching about the remnant is closely linked to the theme of God's covenants. If it were not for those covenants, we would not be talking about any remnant at all! So we will spend a chapter looking at God's covenants in the Bible (for there is more than one). Doing so will help us to answer the question of whether the remnant motif applies to African minorities as well as to the Jewish people.

Once we have settled that point, we can examine the implications of the minority theology we have developed for majorities and minorities in Africa today. Then we can go on to look at what this means for us and for the church today.

It is my prayer that this book will bring encouragement to ministers of the gospel in places where the church is a heavily persecuted minority. In countries like Nigeria, Sudan, Eritrea, and Egypt, for example, the Muslim concept of the *umma* shapes public policy, so that all aspects of life are governed by Muslim law. The decisions that are made often benefit the elites and ignore the needs of the masses, let alone the needs of minorities. In such contexts, African Christians have become disillusioned, despairing and, to some extent, confused. However, we can be encouraged by the fact that even in times and places like these, God still has his saints, a remnant.

I pray too that this book will encourage my brothers and sisters who are part of majority ethnic groups to examine their own attitudes, to reflect on the way their communities treat minorities and to work for a more equitable society that more accurately reflects how God treats human beings.

May the study of our God as the God of the remnant strengthen Christians, both teachers and students, living in Africa's violent conflict-ridden societies. May the ideas explored here keep them afloat spiritually, economically, political, and socially. Our God offers hope for the future!

2

The Remnant Motif in the Scriptures

The history we learn at school and in our communities often focuses on the great deeds of powerful heroes. But God's way of acting in history and recording what he has done is rather different. Yes, there are heroic figures in the Bible, but over and over again, the Bible shows God working through just a few people, who are not strong but weak. In fact, God seems to prefer to work with and through minorities.

From Genesis to Chronicles: God's Work with a Remnant

In the book of Genesis we watch in amazement as he chooses just one man, Abraham, as the one through whom all nations will be blessed. He obeys God as he moves away from all his relatives in Ur. He and his small family are a minority, living as nomads among people who are not like them and with whom they are sometimes in alliances and sometimes in conflict.

We watch this small family grow very slowly. It is only in his old age that his son Isaac is born. Isaac has only two sons, Esau and Jacob, and they are estranged. God chooses to work primarily through only one of them, Jacob. The family grows larger as Jacob has twelve sons. But God's focus falls on just one of these sons – Joseph. Joseph is a mere teenager when he is sold into slavery and finds himself utterly alone in the world, betrayed by his brothers and surrounded by strangers. Yet, strangely, God uses this isolated man to save his family and preserve the line of Abraham in a time of great drought. Strikingly, it is Joseph who first uses the word "remnant" in Scripture. He tells his brothers, "God sent me ahead of you to preserve for you a *remnant* on earth and to save your lives by a great deliverance" (Gen 45:7). Joseph brings his father and his brothers to live in Egypt in the area known as the land of Goshen. But they have little status, for as shepherds they are despised by the Egyptian majority (Gen 46:34). But as their numbers continue to grow, the majority start to perceive this minority group is a threat and deliberately set out to oppress them. They force them into manual labour on projects for the benefit of the majority and deny them proper healthcare, encouraging midwives to allow Hebrew babies to die (Exod 1:6–19).

Yet, amazingly, God continues to work through this oppressed minority. Moses did not mince his words when he told the Israelites, "The LORD did not set his affection on you and choose you because you were more numerous than other peoples, for you were the fewest of all peoples" (Deut 7:7). The books from Exodus to Deuteronomy record how God chooses this group of slaves in Egypt and delivers them from slavery, he leads them into the wilderness where he makes a covenant with them at Sinai and then shapes them into his covenant people, giving them the promised land to be their home. The books of Joshua and Judges then recount how the Israelites settled into the promised land, but their lives were not easy for they were often at the mercy of powerful neighbours and God repeatedly had to deliver them from oppression.

The books of Samuel, Kings and Chronicles record that the Israelites eventually set up a kingdom and erected a great temple in Jerusalem where they could worship God. But these books also tell of how this nation went its own way and grew remote from God. It split into two political factions, eventually setting up two distinct and often warring kingdoms, which oppressed each other when they were not being oppressed by their neighbours or by Egypt, Assyria and Babylon, the superpowers of the ancient world.

While all these troubles were going on, many of those who regarded themselves as true believers were more concerned about observing the rituals of worship than about worshipping the Lord who had not only ordained these rituals but had also commanded them to love and serve him with all their heart and soul (Deut 10:12–13).

The Voices of the Prophets: The Threat and Promise of a Remnant

It is in the context of the two warring kingdoms of Israel and Judah that we hear the Old Testament prophets starting to speak of the threat and promise of a remnant. Each prophet approaches the subject from a slightly different perspective, with some being more positive than others. But they all begin with judgement. Of these prophets, one of the darkest is Amos, who was sent to the northern kingdom of Israel. In light of the severity of Israel's sin and unfaithfulness to the God who had redeemed them from Egypt, Amos pronounced an unremitting message of judgement. He held out no hope of escape: "All the sinners among my people will die by the sword" (Amos 9:10). But in the last five verses of the final chapter of his book, Amos offers the faintest glimmer of hope as God promises that one day he will "restore David's fallen shelter" (Amos 9:11). Is there hope that a remnant will survive?

It is Amos's younger contemporary Isaiah, who prophesied to the southern kingdom of Judah, who expands on what this glimmer of hope means. He was the first to speak at length about the idea of a remnant.

Isaiah foresaw that turbulent times lay head for the nation of Judah. He was called to serve God at a time when the nation was spiritually bankrupt and things were politically, economically, socially, culturally, and spiritually unstable. His message is summed up in the opening chapter of his book, which plainly reveals the nation's moral and spiritual waywardness. In 1:1–9 he accuses Israel of having turned its back on God, with the result that it is experiencing national calamities that only a remnant may survive: "Unless the Lord Almighty had left us some survivors, we would have become like Sodom, we would have been like Gomorrah" (Isa 1:9).

Perhaps surprisingly, this revolt against following God went hand in hand with what Alexander calls "punctilious exactness in religious duties."[1] The behaviour of the priests and people gave the impression that they were worshipping God, but God was not fooled. He knew that such worship counted for nothing (Isa 1:10–20). The chapter ends with verses contrasting the current wicked state of the nation and its future state after God has acted to destroy the wicked and restore righteous rulers (Isa 1:21–31). This future state will come into being because, as God declares later in the book of Isaiah, "my unfailing love for you will not be shaken nor my covenant of peace be removed" (Isa 54:10). God would punish his people, but he would also preserve a remnant of his people.

Both the judgement and the exile lay more than a century in the future when Isaiah prophesied, and the return of the remnant was almost two centuries in the future. But Isaiah had an unshakeable faith that God would act to purify his people and that he would preserve a remnant. He was so convinced of this truth that he not only preached it in person but also acted on his belief when he named his children, as we can tell from the incident recorded in Isaiah 7.

---

1. Joseph Addison Alexander, *Isaiah Translated and Explained* (Grand Rapids: Eerdmans, 1965), 19.

King Ahaz of Judah and his people were terrified because powerful neighbouring kings had formed an alliance against Judah. In this climate of fear, the Lord sent Isaiah to the king with a message that Ahaz should put his faith in God, and warning him of the consequences of not doing so: "If you do not stand firm in your faith, you will not stand at all" (Isa 7:9). But what is striking to us about this message is the two people delivering it. God specifically tells Isaiah that he is not to go alone to see the king: "Go out, you and your son Shear-Jashub, to meet Ahaz" (Isa 7:3). God specifically mentions Isaiah's son by name because the boy's presence will send a symbolic message to the king and to the whole nation. The name Shear-Jashub means "a remnant shall return." His name thus conveyed both a threat and a promise. The threat was that of exile, for the name implied that most of the nation would not survive. The promise offered hope – even if the nation was defeated and apparently wiped out, there would be a remnant and they would return.

Later, commenting on the names of his other children, Isaiah says, "Here am I, and the children the Lord has given me. We are signs and symbols in Israel from the Lord Almighty, who dwells on Mount Zion" (Isa 8:18).

Ahaz ignored Isaiah's warning, for he did not realize that when one grasps who God is and what he is doing in his creation, one can laugh at fear and be unafraid of the future. For, come what may, God will surely leave a remnant that will bear witness to his love, righteousness, mercy, and grace.

The prophecies of Isaiah contain an important lesson for Africa. Isaiah argues with great clarity that God is the Lord of history (Isa 10:22–23). He gave Judah the freedom to choose whether to obey him. He allowed them to refuse to listen and to rely on armaments and warfare rather than on God. But their freedom did not include freedom from the consequences of their choices, as Isaiah points out in a later prophecy:

> Woe to those who go down to Egypt for help,
>   who rely on horses,
> who trust in the multitude of their chariots
>   and in the great strength of their horsemen
> but do not look to the Holy One of Israel,
>   or seek help from the LORD. . . .
> But the Egyptians are mere mortals and not God;
>   their horses are flesh and not spirit.
> When the LORD stretches out his hand,
>   those who help will stumble,
>   those who are helped will fall;
>   all will perish together. (Isa 31:1, 3)

God's people would learn through hard experience that it was foolishness to act in the way they did. The God who can do all things is the only support network that humans need. They do not need to ally themselves with the powerful or with "majority groups." Only after they have come to that awareness, would the survivors return to God in repentance and faith.

This truth is still relevant today. In the ongoing ethnic, political, economic and religious crises in Nigeria and beyond, people foolishly seek solutions in many places, including alliances with political powers and returning to the spiritual powers of African Traditional Religion. There is no hope along that path. The threat of being left a remnant looms large.

But we who believe in the Lord God Almighty can still find solace in God's ability to preserve a remnant and keep them faithfully committed to him. God's purpose of redemption is not thwarted by the indifference of human beings. We can thus also rejoice in the promise that a remnant will indeed survive.

Ezra and Nehemiah: The Preservation and Humility of a Remnant

The people of Israel ignored all the warnings of the prophets, and so they experienced the judgement foretold by Amos, Isaiah and other prophets. First the northern kingdom of Israel fell to the Assyrians who deported most of the population and settled strangers on their land. Then, roughly 130 years later, Babylonian forces marched against the southern kingdom of Judah and besieged Jerusalem, its capital. The last chapters of 2 Kings and Jeremiah dramatically recount its fall as the Babylonians overwhelm the city's defences, enter it and destroy both the city and the temple at its heart. Almost all who survived this disaster were dragged away into exile in Babylon. It appeared that there was no future for the descendants of Abraham, Isaac and Jacob.

But God's judgement, while terrible, was not the end. Jeremiah had foretold – in both a threat and a promise – that "this whole country will become a desolate wasteland, and these nations will serve the king of Babylon seventy years" (Jer 25:11). Israel's defeat did not prove that the Babylonian gods were stronger than the God of Israel – quite the opposite. Working through the politics of ungodly nations, God fulfilled the threat of judgement, and seventy years later he again used the politics of ungodly nations to fulfil his promise that his people would be allowed to return to their homeland. But the number who returned was small in comparison with the number who had left. This is why we describe them as a "remnant." They were the few who had survived.

When Cyrus king of Persia allowed the exiles to return to Jerusalem to rebuild the temple, he did not realize that he was being used to fulfil the prophecies made by Isaiah many years earlier (Isa 44:28). Cyrus believed he was making his own decisions about the reorganization of his kingdom and did not realize that God was working through him to provide for his people. He did not realize that the tiny remnant of the Jewish nation straggling back along the dry, dusty and dangerous route to their ruined capital, Jerusalem, would be used by God. Cyrus did not realize that God's plan stretched far beyond his own reign, or that there would come a day when a courtier serving another king would use his position as cupbearer to get permission to rebuild the walls of Jerusalem. Through that bedraggled remnant who staggered back to Jerusalem, God would fulfil his promises and reveal his love to the world he had created. Through that remnant God would show his sovereignty over all nations and reveal his generous grace, compassion, love, mercy, and patience with his people.

The books of Ezra and Nehemiah tell the story of this remnant. Ezra tells of Cyrus's edict which made this possible, of the temple treasures that were returned to the Jews, of their 800-kilometre journey back to Jerusalem, and of how they started to rebuild. Those are the good stories. But Ezra also tells of the troubles this small group faced. They were persecuted and hindered in every way by those who had moved into the land while they were gone. The prophet Haggai had to remind the discouraged remnant that their very existence showed that "the Lord is still with His people, even as he had covenanted with them when he brought them out of the land of Egypt."[2] Their return from exile was a second exodus, and their rebuilding of the temple symbolized a future with hope. Speaking through Haggai, the Lord promised that even though the rebuilt temple was far inferior to the grand temple Solomon had built and the Babylonians had destroyed, this was not the final temple. In due time he would send "what is desired by all nations" and fill his house with glory so that "the glory of this present house will be greater than the glory of the former house . . . and in this place I will grant peace" (Hag 2:9).

God's promise of peace in the future did not remove the real dangers of the present. The remnant who had returned were very vulnerable to attack, for as Nehemiah told King Artaxerxes, "the wall of Jerusalem is broken down, and its gates have been burned with fire" (Neh 1:3). Their city was not only unsafe, it was also a cause for shame. So Nehemiah requested the king's permission to return to Jerusalem and rebuild the wall. Once the temple and the city walls

---

2. E. J. Young, *An Introduction to the Old Testament* (Grand Rapids: Eerdmans, 1984), 293.

had been rebuilt, the returned exiles, led by Ezra and Nehemiah, gathered to hear the law of God read aloud, to confess their sins, and to renew the covenant (Neh 8:1–13:31). We will consider the topic of covenants in the next chapter.

Because Ezra and Nehemiah believed in the possibility of a holy seed, a remnant, they were able to help the returned exiles rediscover their faith and return to fellowship with God. They pointed the remnant to the real source of life and tranquillity both for this life and for the life to come. They helped the remnant to rise above their fears and their shame to do a great work for the Lord. They helped the returnees to align their world view with God's future purposes for Israel and for the entire human race.

As leaders, both Ezra and Nehemiah knew that it was only by the grace of God that they and those around them had survived the exile and been able to return to their land. Ezra the scribe knew that he was one of the few survivors who was in a position to teach the people. Surely this was the catalyst that led him to commit himself to studying, obeying, and teaching the law to Israel (Ezra 7:10). Through that work he would bring honour and glory to God.

Meanwhile Nehemiah knew that he owed his position to God, who had given him favour with King Artaxerxes and enabled him to return to rebuild the wall of Jerusalem. In full awareness of this, he did his utmost to honour God by carrying out his administrative duties with honesty, integrity, justice and righteousness. Modelling his behaviour on God's generous grace, he forfeited his entitlements and privileges for the benefit of others (Neh 5:14–18). He listened to the people's concerns and did not hesitate to challenge the unethical behaviour of powerful men and officials in his own administration: "When I heard their outcry and these charges, I was very angry. I pondered them in my mind and then accused the nobles and officials. I told them, . . . 'What you are doing is not right. Shouldn't you walk in the fear of our God to avoid the reproach of our Gentile enemies?'" (Neh 5:6–9).

Like Ezra, Nehemiah did not look for an earthly reward from human beings but relied instead on God. That is why the book that is named after him ends with the words, "Remember me with favour, my God" (Neh 13:31). Similar words are found in four other places in the book (Neh 5:19; 13:14, 22, 29–30). His reliance on God to reward him helped him overcome the temptations of leadership, which include being trapped in the coils of human pride and self-importance.

Too often when individuals or groups attain some kind of power in a situation, they forget their values and become uncaring and inhumane. Instead of using their position to ensure that love, justice, and fairness thrive, they focus on their own status. Nehemiah did not do this. Despite all that had been achieved in Jerusalem (the rebuilding of the city walls, the restoration of the exiles, the re-institution of temple worship) and despite being the official representative of the most powerful king in the world of that time, Nehemiah is remembered for humbly focusing on pleasing God.

Reflecting on Nehemiah's life should lead us to alter our behaviour. We too are not entitled to the things we enjoy; everything we have has been given to us by God. In that sense, we are no different from the remnant who returned to Jerusalem. When we truly grasp this idea, we will start to live differently and will focus on pleasing God.

We will also be more aware of our own sin and why we do not deserve the blessings we have. Nehemiah and Ezra knew that the exile was primarily caused by their ancestors' rebellion against God's revealed will and purpose, and therefore they led the returned exiles in confession, renouncing the shameful and rebellious ways of their forebears. We have a record of this prayer in Nehemiah 9. In it the remnant confessed both how sinful they were and how God's faithfulness had never wavered. Recognition of God's mercy and faithfulness led them to rededicate themselves to God. Nehemiah then documented their commitment and asked them to sign it to ensure that they would always remember the past and to prevent them from breaking their commitment in the future (Neh 10:1–39). Through the work of these leaders, the returned exiles humbly reaffirmed their love for God and their willingness to pay allegiance to him alone (Neh 10:28–29).

Paul: God's Grace and Mercy to a Remnant

You might think that the idea of the remnant would largely have been forgotten by New Testament times. Yet although he lived five hundred years after Ezra and Nehemiah, Paul also knew what it was like to be part of a minority group controlled by a world power, for what had once been the sovereign Jewish nation was now reduced to merely a small province in the vast Roman Empire. Paul was also aware that political forces were not the only oppressors. So in his letters he reminded his readers that since Satan's rebellion, our struggle is against "the rulers, against the authorities, against the powers of this dark world and against the spiritual forces of evil in the heavenly realms" (Eph 6:12). These powers and principalities seek to manipulate and mobilize human structures, systems, institutions, and organizations and use them to wage war against God and his people.

Yet Paul is not discouraged, for he clings to the glorious truth of the remnant. After reminding his readers of how God had preserved a faithful remnant in the days of Elijah, he says, "so too, at the present time there is a remnant chosen by grace" (Rom 11:5). In that passage, he is referring specifically to his Jewish contemporaries who had chosen to follow Christ. But Paul's understanding of who comprised the remnant did not limit the concept to Jews. He would have known that the Old Testament contains many passages like the one below, in which God speaks of his plan to include non-Jews in his blessings on the remnant.

> "To the eunuchs who keep my Sabbaths,
>   who choose what pleases me
>   and hold fast to my covenant –
> to them I will give within my temple and its walls
>   a memorial and a name
>   better than sons and daughters;
> I will give them an everlasting name
>   that will endure forever.
> And foreigners who bind themselves to the LORD
>   to minister to him,
> to love the name of the LORD,
>   and to be his servants,
> all who keep the Sabbath without desecrating it
>   and who hold fast to my covenant –
> these I will bring to my holy mountain
>   and give them joy in my house of prayer.
> Their burnt offerings and sacrifices
>   will be accepted on my altar;
> for my house will be called
>   a house of prayer for all nations."
> The Sovereign LORD declares –
>   he who gathers the exiles of Israel:
> "I will gather still others to them
>   besides those already gathered." (Isa 56:4–8)

Paul brings this idea to the forefront as he reminds his readers that God had reached out to include Gentiles in his faithful people; they too are now part of this remnant. The Gentiles are like branches of a wild olive tree that have been grafted onto the root of a cultivated olive tree, where they now flourish alongside the original branches (Rom 11:17–24). As Paul explains in Romans 9:8: "It is not the children by physical descent who are God's children, but it is the children of the promise who are regarded as Abraham's offspring." These "children of the promise" are all those who are like Abraham in believing God's covenant promises (Rom 4:13–25).

Paul understood that the remnant is an outward demonstration of God's faithfulness not just to the Jews but to the whole human race, and especially to those who believe in Christ and constitute the spiritual Israel (or what he calls "the Israel of God" – Gal 6:16). The new covenant that Christ established revealed that God's promises include the entire human race – male and female, majority ethnic groups and minority ethnic groups, Jews and Gentiles. The Jews were making a mistake if they thought of themselves as the only remnant (Rom 9:24–25).

Paul knows that there is nothing in the whole created universe, including human sin and rebellion, that is capable of thwarting God's sovereign plan. The fact that the majority of the nation of Israel did not accept Jesus as the Messiah did not cause God to discard Israel. There is a remnant, which is being saved through faith in Jesus Christ whom they recognize as the Messiah. This is why Paul can confidently claim that nothing in all creation "will be able to separate us from the love of God" (Rom 8:39). The remnant of believers from the Jewish community is united in the body of Christ with those few from the Gentile community who believe.

The language of the remnant permeates Paul's writing as he calls on Christians to remember God's generous grace and mercy. He knows that none of us is entitled to membership in God's family. We all stand under his judgement. But in his grace and mercy, God has restored us to a right standing with him, just as he restored the people of Israel to the land he had promised them. As a remnant, we can rely on God to preserve us. That is why, despite the hardships which he and his team faced as a minority in a hostile world (2 Cor 4:8–10), Paul could write:

> Who shall separate us from the love of Christ? Shall trouble or hardship or persecution or famine or nakedness or danger or sword? . . . No, in all these things we are more than conquerors through him who loved us. For I am convinced that neither death nor life, neither angels nor demons, neither the present nor the future, nor any powers, neither height nor depth, nor anything else in all creation, will be able to separate us from the love of God that is in Christ Jesus our Lord. (Rom 8:35–39)

Like Nehemiah, Paul understood his tremendous debt and fearful responsibility to the Lord. Like Nehemiah, he did his utmost to live in a way that brought honour to God. So in writing to his critics in Corinth, he could say this:

> Our conscience testifies that we have conducted ourselves in the world, and especially in our relations with you, with integrity and godly sincerity. We have done so, relying not on worldly wisdom but on God's grace. (2 Cor 1:12)

Many Christian do not think, live, or act like Paul. They are prepared to manipulate others and avoid confronting evil because they value the privileges of leadership and the opinions of their supporters more than they value God's approval. They are not prepared to suffer for what they believe. Only those who recognize that they are not superior, that they have no status other than what they have received from God can live as he did. Only they are truly part of the faithful remnant.

3

Remnants Today

We have seen that in Isaiah and Nehemiah the biblical word "remnant" is used to refer to those who are the survivors of God's judgement. In that sense, it is associated primarily with the sins of Israel's ancestors, as the people acknowledge in the prayer recorded in Nehemiah 9 (see Neh 9:16–17, 26, 29, 34–35). But we are wrong if we focus solely on the sins and assume that the remnant deserve their suffering. If we do that, we put ourselves on higher moral ground so that we can look down on them. Yet if we are honest, we must admit that our ancestors, and we ourselves, deserve the same judgement. We have little to be proud of in the way we have conducted ourselves. We too have turned our backs on God's law. We have no grounds for claiming that we deserve his favour.

We might do better to look at the remnant from a different perspective: they are the ones who have survived because of God's mercy. This theme too comes through strongly in Nehemiah 9, where the people acknowledge that "in your great mercy you did not put an end to them or abandon them, for you are a gracious and merciful God" (Neh 9:31; see also Neh 9:19–21, 27). This was the element of remnant theology that Paul focused on in his letter to the Romans when he spoke of the Gentile and Jewish believers as a remnant saved by faith.

In Deuteronomy God warned the Israelites that if they turned away from him and disobeyed him, "only a few of you will survive" (Deut 4:27). Israel was not able to survive in its own strength. Nor can we. We all survive only because God has constantly demonstrated his great power in the affairs of the world throughout history. This truth was not only revealed to Israel, it was also known to other nations:

The remnant idea is present in Sumerian, Akkadian, Hittite, Ugaritic, and Egyptian cultures in a large variety of genres, such

17

as myth, legend, epic, prophecy, prayer, hymn, letter, and annal. It appears with such human entities as individual, family, clan, tribe, army, nation, and mankind as a whole. The large variety of mortal threats in the natural, social, and political spheres emphasizes the common denominator of the respective remnant notions, namely man's existential concern to preserve life when endangered by mortal threats. A remnant means life and continued existence through innate potentialities of renewal and restoration.[1]

The concept of a remnant is also part of Africa's history, as I know from my own experience. When I started my pastoral ministry in 1985, I was sent to pastor a church that was located in the vicinity of an ethnic group whose account of their own history says that their ancestors once lived near Jema'a in what is now Kaduna State in Nigeria. However, these ancestors committed such atrocities and were so evil that they invited God's judgement. They were struck down by a plague, and all those who stayed in their traditional area died. The only ones who survived were those who escaped to the territory where I came to know them. They still regarded themselves as a remnant who had survived the judgement on their people.

All of these different accounts of the survival of minorities remind us that this world can be a dangerous place where few survive and flourish. The danger may take different forms. It may be our physical life that is threatened, or it may be our social life, political life, economic life, or our spiritual life. Some people succumb to these threats, but in God's mercy a remnant remain.

Survivors of Trauma

When we come to understand the concept of a remnant as referring to those who survive disaster, we find ourselves able to identify many different kinds of remnants – although today we would probably call them "survivors." You may see yourself in one of these groups:

- *Survivors of personal trauma*: Some of us have survived life-threatening challenges that have left us scarred, reduced from what we were or might have become. The challenges may have been physical – a snake bite, cancer, a stroke, loss of vision, a head injury. They may be emotional scars as we live with the memory of

---

1. G. F. Hasel, "Remnant," in *The Interpreter's Dictionary of the Bible*, Supplementary Volume, Keith Grim, ed. (Nashville: Abingdon, 1984), 735–36.

traumatic experiences like watching people die after being bitten by a dog infected with rabies. They may be social losses as we mourn the fact that we and others were deprived of opportunities for education. Yet, by the grace of God, we are the remnant who have survived these traumas.

- *Survivors of family trauma*: Some of us come from dysfunctional or devastated families. God rescued us from the devastation that other family members experienced in order to preserve a witness for his name. This was the case with Joseph, whose relationship with his brothers was marred by favouritism and jealousy that exploded into violent abduction (Gen 45:7). Like him, you may have been saved to preserve a remnant.

- *Survivors of natural disasters*: Others among us have survived natural disasters such as drought, floods, crop failures and famine, hailstorms, earthquakes, mudslides, wildfires, and pandemic diseases such as Ebola and COVID-19. Whole villages have been wiped out, yet God has miraculously preserved a few.

- *Survivors of peer pressure*: Some people who are serving God today were once part of groups that encouraged harmful lifestyles such as drunkenness, drug addiction, gangsterism, and sexual immorality. Many of their peers who refused to change have passed away, but God rescued a remnant and transformed them, keeping them alive as a remnant through his mercy.

- *Survivors of wars*: Africa has known many wars. In Nigeria, for example, people who lived through the Biafran War can testify that they are a remnant of the more than one million who lost their lives in that war. Yet God preserved them for himself.

- *Survivors of terrorism*: Africa is home to a number of destructive terrorist groups. Among the deadliest are Boko Haram in Nigeria and al-Shabaab in Somalia and Kenya. These groups destroy human lives and property, and leave many maimed for life. Those who survive their raids know what it is to be a suffering remnant.

- *Survivors of sexual trauma*: Some of us may also have experienced sexual abuse. There are daughters who have been physically abused by their fathers or other family members – often over a long period. There are wives who have been treated as mere possessions and from whom sexual favours have been demanded without regard for their feelings or their physical state at that time. Other women carry physical and emotional scars after being raped by militias. Nor is it only women who experience sexual trauma, although women may be in the majority in this category. There are men and boys who have known the humiliation of rape. Those who have endured sexual trauma relive this experience over and over again. They know what it is to suffer, but they know too that they have been preserved by the grace of God.

Minority Ethnic Groups

All the above examples focus primarily on the experience of individuals who have survived disasters. But there is also another category of the remnant that we need to remember today, one that is possibly even more closely allied to the biblical story. There are groups who constitute a remnant because they are part of small people groups that are greatly outnumbered by other groups in their society, just as the Jews were vastly outnumbered by the Egyptians and the Babylonians.

In many societies there are majority groups who assume that merely because they are in the majority they are socially, intellectually, politically and economically superior to all others in the society. This belief is found across the world, and causes great suffering wherever it is found. But it is particularly dangerous in Africa with its multitude of ethnic groups. Nigeria alone has four major ethnic groups: the Hausa, Fulani, Yoruba and Igbo as well as more than 490 smaller ethnic groups; the Democratic Republic of Congo has 250 ethnic groups; South Africa has 224 ethnic groups; Cameroon has 140; Ethiopia has 80; Egypt has 22; Uganda has 17; and Malawi has 6.[2] The list could go on and on. What all these African countries have in common is that some ethnic groups constitute majorities while others are minorities. And in most cases, the minorities are treated as second-class citizens.

What do I mean by this statement? To explain it, let me point out that different ethnic groups are seldom treated equally. Majority ethnic groups cling to their political and economic hegemony and act as overlords, while minority groups are relegated to the background or assigned "spare-tyre status." Minorities are treated as if their only role is to help the majority maintain the status quo. When minorities resist this role, they are often demonized and abused. Regardless of their constitutional status, they seldom enjoy the same rights as citizens from majority ethnic groups. Some are even made to feel like strangers in their own homeland. As the Catholic bishop of Sokoto,

---

2. Information drawn from national websites.

Matthew Hassan Kukah, said: "Victims of discrimination in Nigeria experience it because they belong to the wrong clan, ethnic group, gender or religion."[3] What this means in practice is that someone's value and worth is determined on the basis of the size of their ethnic group. Sadly this situation does not only apply in society: it also applies in the church, which too often acts as if ethnic minorities are not as important as the majority ethnic group in God's eyes.

Minority ethnic groups have often resigned themselves to their fate as second-class citizens. Not only that, but they buy into the system that oppresses them and look down on others who are designated as belonging to another minority group. In other words, minority groups find ways to look down on their fellow minorities!

My understanding of these matters has been sharpened by my own experiences as a member of a minority group in my own country of Nigeria, where the majority dominates every aspect of the life of a nation. I have seen how the thirst for political and economic power has demonized our fellow human beings from other groups. All of us, whether we come from majorities or minorities, are blinded by our own social, political, intellectual, and economic achievements and the assessments of others. We fail to see that we are neither superior nor inferior to others, but that like all human beings we are beset with weaknesses.

Minority Religious Groups

In Africa, and around the world, there is often a close correlation between particular ethnic groups and particular religious affiliations. For example, in India, much of the population is Hindu; in Northern Nigeria, the majority of the Fulani are Muslim. But among these groups there are minority ethnic groups who follow different religions. So there are minority groups in northern Nigeria that identify themselves as Christian rather than Muslim. To give another example, the Middle Belt Region of Nigeria is inhabited by several ethnic groups. A number of the smaller groups resisted Usman Dan Fodio's jihad of 1804 that tried to convert them from African Traditional Religion to Islam. These groups did, however, embrace Christianity when it was introduced to the Middle Belt at a later stage. The Hausa-Fulani majority group responded by marginalizing these people groups and denying them access to political and economic power, both in the region and in the nation. Similar examples could

---

3. Mathew Hassan Kukah, *The Church and the Politics of Social Responsibility* (Ikate-Surulere, Lagos: Sovereign Prints, 2007), 40.

be given from across Africa. When a minority ethnic group is also a religious minority, the oppression they experience is intensified.

The situation is even more difficult for individuals who change their religious affiliation. Muslims who convert to Christianity may be expelled from their communities and families, and many find themselves living among Christians who do not understand their loneliness and their traumas. They may well find themselves feeling like the remnant of the Israelites enduring exile and scorn.

Minorities within the Church

In some areas of Africa, Christians form a majority and the churches are crowded. Unfortunately, those who are thronging these churches are sometimes less interested in faithful discipleship than in maintaining the status quo. They are like the people of Isaiah's day in that they are happy to carry out religious rituals without any attempt to align their values with Christ's values. Those who speak out for the truth and who challenge injustice and oppression soon discover that they are a minority. They endure the scorn of those who have come to power by supporting the status quo and may suffer physical, emotional, and economic abuse. They may be forced out of office and even out of churches. In many respects, they will share the same minority status as the Old Testament prophets.

Hope for Remnants

We can never fully understand God's purposes in allowing the many different types of suffering described above, and we should never presume to tell survivors why they have suffered, as if we know God's mind. God warned against such thinking in Isaiah, when he said, "my thoughts are not your thoughts, neither are your ways my ways" (Isa 55:8).

But what we can hold out to survivors is the hope expressed in the words of Scripture. We have already considered some of these words in the previous chapter. However, the truth is repeated again and again. Many of the Old Testament prophets, for instance, used the image of a scattered flock in association with the idea of a remnant. So Jeremiah spoke of a time when "he who scattered Israel will gather them and will watch over his flock like a shepherd" (Jer 31:10). Isaiah spoke of the Lord gathering the scattered remnant of Israel:

> He will raise a banner for the nations
>> and gather the exiles of Israel;
> he will assemble the scattered people of Judah
>> from the four quarters of the earth. (Isa 11:12)

Jesus himself often used metaphors involving sheep. He described the crowds of people who came to him as "harassed and helpless, like sheep without a shepherd" (Matt 9:36; Mark 6:34) and described himself as the Good Shepherd who would care for the remnant of a scattered flock, while also reaching out to "other sheep that are not of this sheep pen" (John 10:14–16). He also spoke of his earthly ministry as focused on "the lost sheep of Israel" (Matt 10:6), a phrase that would have reminded his hearers of the Lord's words to Ezekiel: "As a shepherd looks after his scattered flock when he is with them, so will I look after my sheep. I will rescue them from all the places where they were scattered on a day of clouds and darkness" (Ezek 34:12).

This remnant motif which reoccurs in Scripture assures us all that our survival is not an accident. You and I were saved by the power of God, and for the purposes of God.

But how can I be so certain of that? How could Isaiah, Nehemiah, Paul and the prophets have been so sure that a remnant would survive and was surviving? How could they build their lives on that certainty? And how can I apply what they had to say to ancient Israel to life in Africa today? Surely that is taking the concept of the remnant a step too far?

The answer to those questions, which have to be taken seriously, is rooted in our understanding of the covenants of God. That is why we will spend the next chapter looking at those covenants.

4

Remnants and God's Covenant Love

Isaiah, Nehemiah, Ezra, and Paul were confident that a remnant would survive, and was surviving. Their confidence was not rooted simply in a revelation each of them had received as an individual. Rather, they were all building on their knowledge of God's character as revealed in the historical covenants he had made with the beings he had created.

As we examine these covenants, we will discover that God did not only make covenants with the Jews, as we sometimes believe. His covenants have important implications for believers in general, and for minorities around the world, including in Africa. We will gain new confidence to join with Paul in his answer to the questions at the start of his letter to the Romans: "After all, is God the God of Jews only? Isn't he also the God of Gentiles?" Like Paul, we will be able to answer, "Of course he is" (Rom 3:29 NLT).

The Concept of a Covenant

The idea of a covenant "is undeniably a major theological motif in the Bible as a whole. The Hebrew term itself (*berit*) is found some eighty-two times in the Pentateuch alone and is used to describe both interpersonal and divine-human covenants."[1] It can even be said that "covenant is a central concept in the theological ethics of the Hebrew Scriptures."[2]

---

1. Paul R. Williamson, "Covenant," in *Dictionary of the Old Testament: Pentateuch* (Downers Grove, IL: InterVarsity, 2003), 139.

2. Glen H. Stassen and David P. Gushee, *Kingdom Ethics: Following Jesus in Contemporary Contexts* (Downers Grove, IL: InterVarsity Press, 2003), 293.

But what exactly is a covenant? The simplest definition is that it is an agreement between two parties. A more complex definition is that it is "a solemn commitment guaranteeing promises or obligations undertaken by one or both covenanting parties."[3] The reference to "promises . . . undertaken by one or both covenanting parties" also brings out an important distinction: there are two basic types of covenants: conditional and unconditional covenants. In conditional covenants, if either party fails to fulfil its obligations, the covenant is broken. In unconditional covenants, the obligation holds whatever the other party does.

This, of course, brings us to the very important question: What type of covenants has God entered into with humanity? Are his promises to us conditional on what we do, or are they unconditional? And there is, of course, the further question: What has this to do with the remnant and with minorities? And this leads us to yet another question: If God's covenants were with the Jewish nation, what is their relevance to Africans? To answer those questions, we need to look more closely at the covenants recorded in Scripture.

The Nature of God's Covenants

Our God is a dynamic God! Over the course of human history, he has made more than one covenant. The first was with Adam and all living creatures (Gen 1–2). The second was with Noah and all living creatures (Gen 6:18; 8:22; 9:8–17). The third was with Abraham and his descendants on behalf of the rest of humanity (Gen 12:2–3; 15:17). The fourth was the Mosaic or Sinai covenant that is connected to the Abrahamic covenant, particularly in terms of the response that God expects from Israel. Fifth, there was the Davidic covenant, and, finally, there is the new covenant inaugurated by Christ's death on the cross.

What is striking about these covenants is that in the majority of them God entered into a covenant with an individual, but the content of the covenant extends well beyond that individual. That is why many of the covenants have two parts: the particular and the universal.

The Covenant with Adam

The author of Genesis asserts, "In the beginning, God created the heavens and the earth" (Gen 1:1). The biblical narrative of the creation is the wonderful story of God's expression of his love for the people he created and for the

---

3. Williamson, "Covenant," 139.

whole earth. God spoke and the world sprang into life. Out of love, God made everything that exists, filling this planet with all kinds of creatures. Human beings stood out among these creatures because they were given the ability to think and reason.

God entered into a covenant giving Adam and Eve stewardship of the natural world (Gen 2:16–17). In a loving, covenant relationship, God handed over the earth that he had made to humans so that they could care for it and watch over its well-being.

Of course, humans then as now struggled to recognize God's love and mandate because there was an enemy who was determined to wreck God's plans. The enemy has always been jealous of God's love and covenant with humankind. Smarter than humans, he succeeded in making Eve and Adam doubt God's sincerity and commitment to the covenant relationship God had established with them. Once they doubted God's love for them, they disobeyed God and plunged headlong into an incomparably great fall. Their desire to be independent, to be their own bosses, resulted in their being cut off from God.

But in spite of their sin, God did not end his creation covenant with them or with us as their descendants. The whole of creation is still beautiful in God's sight, for he knew that he had made it "good" and "very good" (Gen 1:10, 31). He continued his covenant of love, despite human disobedience and the fall. God takes covenant-keeping seriously, and he was determined to continue to love the world and to save it from self-destruction (John 3:16). The fact that the eternal God will keep his covenant relationship with his creation is a source of hope for us.

But it is also a source of responsibility. Human beings – all human beings – are still made in God's image, and we are all still expected to be responsible for creation. Our task is more difficult because of Adam and Eve's disobedience, but nevertheless this unconditional covenant continues to hold for all their descendants – including their African descendants – right up to the present day. All of us, minorities and majorities, have a responsibility to care for the creation that God has entrusted to us. And we should never forget that God's creation includes our fellow human beings – all of them, whether they come from minority or majority groups.

The Covenant with Noah

God's love for his creation does not mean that he will not judge it. When human sinfulness reached the point of no return because people were addicted to violence, God took action and exposed their vulnerability. He sent a flood to wipe them all out. But in his covenant love he did not destroy every human being; he preserved Noah and his family, a tiny remnant of humanity, as well as many other living creatures.

After the flood had receded, God entered into a covenant with Noah:

> And God said, "This is the sign of the covenant I am making between me and you and *every living creature*, a covenant for all generations to come: I have set my rainbow in the clouds, and it will be the sign of the covenant between me and the earth. Whenever I bring clouds over the earth and the rainbow appears in the clouds, I will remember my covenant between me and you *and all living creatures* of every kind. Never again will the waters become a flood to destroy all life. Whenever the rainbow appears in the clouds, I will see it and remember the everlasting covenant between God and all *living creatures* of every kind on the earth."
>
> So God said to Noah, "This is the sign of the covenant I have established between me and *all life* on the earth." (Gen 9:12–17)

The words I have italicized all repeat the same idea and are clearly important. Christopher Wright describes the covenant with Noah in these terms:

> It is explicitly a commitment by God to the whole of his creation, to all life on earth – not just the human race, but every living creature. It comes in two parts – first of all, God's promise to preserve Noah in the midst of the judgement of the flood, and then, after the flood, God's commitment is extended to all humans and all creatures. . . .
>
> The Noachic covenant teaches us God's providence. It is not limited to a particular people or a particular place. It emphatically includes all life in the whole earth.[4]

The covenant with Noah has implications for uncountable generations of Noah's descendants:

> As long as the earth endures,
> Seedtime and harvest,
> cold and heat,
> summer and winter,
> day and night,
> will never cease. (Gen 8:22)

---

4. Christopher J. H. Wright, *Knowing God – The Trilogy: Knowing Jesus, God the Father, and the Holy Spirit through the Old Testament* (Carlisle, UK: Langham Global Library, 2017), 73–74.

The fact that we all benefit from the covenant with Noah lends credence to the assurance that, because of his creational covenant of love, God did not give up on the human race. He demonstrated that by leaving a remnant then and now.

The flood illustrated God's utter displeasure with humanity for breaking the universal covenant he had made with Adam and Eve, the representatives of the human race. Yet even after God entered into a new covenant with Noah, humanity did not fare well. Therefore, in what looks like starting all over again, God entered into a covenant with Abraham.

The Covenant with Abraham

God's covenants are always based on grace rather than human deserving, and they are not restricted to the one person with whom the covenant is made. Thus although God's covenant with Abraham focused on God's establishing a particular relationship with Abraham's descendants, the Jews, it has a universal implication.

> I will make you into a great nation,
>   and I will bless you;
> I will make your name great,
>   and you will be a blessing.
> I will bless those who bless you,
>   and whoever curses you I will curse;
> and all peoples of the earth
>   will be blessed through you. (Gen 12:2–3)

This covenant can be described as "the basis of God's redemptive work within human history. The universal goal of this covenant is to bring God's redemptive blessing to all nations . . . People of every nation will share in the blessing covenanted to and through Abraham."[5] God blesses one person (definitely a minority!) so that that person becomes the catalyst and a conduit of God's blessings to the rest of humanity and the entire creation. Christ's incarnation, the virgin birth, as well as his ministry, trial, suffering, death, burial, and resurrection were all part of the package of the Abrahamic covenant.

The Covenant with Moses and the People of Israel at Sinai

The Bible is a book of covenant revelation. In Exodus God reveals himself as the covenant-redeemer of Israel through the mighty miracles he performed

---

5. Wright, *Knowing God*, 75.

on behalf of the Israelites in Egypt and on their way to the promised land. On the basis of that miraculous deliverance, God made himself the basis of Israel's moral, economic, political and social roadmap of life. But the law he gave them as part of his covenant with them was not intended only for their benefit; it was also to be a model for the surrounding nations:

> See, I have taught you decrees and laws as the LORD my God commanded me, so that you may follow them in the land you are entering to take possession of it. Observe them carefully, for this will show your wisdom and understanding to the nations, who will hear about all these decrees and say, "Surely this great nation is a wise and understanding people." What other nation is so great as to have their gods near them the way the LORD our God is near us whenever we pray to him? And what other nation is so great as to have such righteous decrees and laws as this body of laws I am setting before you today? (Deut 4:5–8)

The covenant at Sinai was thus another step along the route to sharing God's blessing with the entire human race.

In terms of our focus on minorities in this book, it is worth noting again what God had to say about Israel, the nation that he has chosen:

> The LORD did not set his affection on you and choose you because you were more numerous than other peoples, for you were the fewest of all peoples. But it was because the LORD loved you and kept the oath he swore to your ancestors that he brought you out with a mighty hand and redeemed you from the land of slavery, from the power of Pharaoh king of Egypt. Know therefore that the LORD your God is God; he is the faithful God, keeping his covenant of love to a thousand generations of those who love him and keep his commandments. (Deut 7:7–9)

God's words make it very clear that it was a minority, not a majority, who were to become the source of blessing to the world. An implicit principle is that God does not want to give us room for pride. He uses a minority group so that the glory will still remain with him.

The Covenant with David

God's covenant with David is described in 2 Samuel 7. The key words are these:

> The LORD declares to you that the LORD himself will establish a house for you: When your days are over and you rest with your

ancestors, I will raise up your offspring to succeed you, your own flesh and blood, and I will establish his kingdom. He is the one who will build a house for my Name, and I will establish the throne of his kingdom forever. I will be his father, and he will be my son. When he does wrong, I will punish him with a rod wielded by men, with floggings inflicted by human hands. But my love will never be taken away from him, as I took it away from Saul, whom I removed from before you. Your house and your kingdom will endure forever before me; your throne will be established forever. (2 Sam 7:11–16)

David responds to these words with amazement, and with a humble prayer:

Who am I, Sovereign LORD, and what is my family, that you have brought me this far? And as if this were not enough in your sight, Sovereign LORD, you have also spoken about the future of the house . . . Sovereign LORD, you are God! Your covenant is trustworthy. (2 Sam 7:18–19, 28)

Whereas the covenant at Sinai focused on the obligations of the Israelites, this covenant with David is not subject to any condition.[6] It is a sign of God's favour to an individual who came from one of the minority tribes of Israel and who was the youngest, and thus the least important, in his family (1 Sam 16:11).

Later kings described God's covenant with David as "a covenant of salt" (2 Chr 13:5). Salt was a preservative, and so this saying meant that this covenant would not decay. It would be permanent (Lev 2:13; Num 18:19). God did promise to discipline those of David's descendants who did wrong, but he would never wipe them out. We see what this means in practice when we read that King Jehoram of Judah, "did evil in the eyes of the LORD. Nevertheless, because of the covenant the Lord had made with David, the Lord was not willing to destroy the house of David. He had promised to maintain a lamp for him and his descendants forever" (2 Chr 21:6–7).

In the same way, when Israel failed in its covenant relationship with God the nation came under God's judgement. The people were carried away into exile in Babylon. Yet, no matter what Israel as a nation did, God was not willing to destroy them completely because of the covenants he had entered into with Abraham, Moses, and David. God made sure that a remnant would survive.

---

6. Riemann, "Covenant," in *The Interpreter's Dictionary of the Bible*, 188–197.

The New Covenant

The whole biblical history of sin, punishment, forgiveness, and restoration reflects the unfolding of God's covenants, which can be seen as essentially one covenant progressively revealed. His first covenant with Adam and Eve revealed his good plans for the human race. His second covenant with Noah, whom God had saved from the flood, further revealed God's plans for the salvation of the world he created. Then God called Abraham, as part of his plan that through Abraham's descendants he would bring salvation to a world that had been corrupted by sin. That plan continued as God called on the Israelites to be his people, and chose the family of David as the root from which the Saviour would come. Jesus Christ was the final embodiment of God's covenant plan. At the last meal he ate with his disciples before his crucifixion, we are told that "he took the cup, saying, 'This cup is the new covenant in my blood, which is poured out for you'" (Luke 22:20). He was instituting the new and final covenant foretold by the prophet Jeremiah

> "This is the covenant I will make with the people of Israel
>   after that time," declares the LORD.
> "I will put my law in their minds
>   and write it on their hearts.
> I will be their God,
>   and they will be my people.
> No longer will they teach their neighbour,
>   or say to one another, 'Know the LORD,'
> because they will all know me,
>   from the least of them to the greatest,"
>   declares the LORD.
> "For I will forgive their wickedness
>   and will remember their sins no more." (Jer 31:33–34)

By shedding his blood for the forgiveness of sins, Jesus guaranteed salvation and opened the door to eternal life.

Jesus also referenced the covenant motif when he appointed twelve disciples, mirroring the twelve tribes of Israel with whom God had made a covenant at Sinai. But in the new covenant that Jesus inaugurated, it was not the physical descendants of the disciples who became the new people of God. Nor was it their relatives or people from their ethnic group who became the church. Only a handful of the Jews welcomed Christ into their lives. Rather, the disciples became the seed of a new covenant people of God, drawn from every nation, united by their faith in Jesus Christ, a faith that became the seed of the church, the body of Christ in which "there is neither Jew nor Gentile, neither slave nor free, nor is there male and female, for you are all one in Christ Jesus" (Gal 3:28).

Conclusion

There can be no doubt that the covenants described in the Bible include other groups of people and do not apply only to the nation of Israel. God's covenant with Abraham was all-embracing, for it includes the blessing of all nations through him and his seed (Gen 12:2–3). God's covenant with Noah shows that despite humankind's inclination to go astray, God refuses to abandon the human race. Although God had every reason to do so, he refused to destroy them.

Given that the covenants apply to people outside the nation of Israel, so too does the idea of a remnant. In both the Old Testament and the New Testament, the "remnant" are those who have somehow escaped God's wrath and judgement on those who have trampled his covenant revelation under their feet. That includes Christians today. They have received God's mercy and find God's grace to help in times of trouble (Heb 4:16). We are all vessels that God is using to bring him glory as we complete his programme for the whole world.

The church is thus a remnant, a visible, historical, organized body characterized by obedience to the commandments of God and rejoicing in the gospel of Christ. When evil strikes, people may reject their faith, but evil cannot destroy the remnant. War or conflict may strip victims of all control over their situations and some may drift away from God's revealed truth, but members of his remnant remain brave and steadfast in their commitment to their covenant God who will be faithful to them.

But if the church is a remnant, and if God's covenants also apply to us, what does this mean for how we live today? That is the topic of the next chapter.

5

Implications of Covenant Theology

God's covenants are not merely ancient history. They have important implications for all of us today. If you doubt this, listen to the words of John Piper:

> The reason God's covenants with Noah, Abraham, Moses, and David ought to increase the joy of our faith is that in all of them the main point is that God exerts all his omnipotence and all his omniscience to do good to his people, and we are that people if we follow Christ in the obedience of faith. The most practical truths any Christian can know are that God is all-powerful, all-wise, and all for you. Nothing will have a more crucial practical impact on the way you use your money, spend your leisure, pursue your vocation, rear children, deal with conflict, or handle anxiety, than a heartfelt confidence that the sovereign God is working everything together for your good out of sheer grace.[1]

With that reminder ringing in our ears, we need to look more at what it means to "follow Christ in the obedience of faith." A good starting point might be to say that as God's children, we are to become like our Christ, our older brother (Rom 8:29). Given that Christ is the "exact representation" of God (Heb 1:3), becoming like Christ also means becoming like God and modelling our characters on his character. But how do we know God's character? We know it through what he has revealed about himself. Part of this revelation is in the

---

1. John Piper, "God's Covenant with David," in *Desiring God: Meditation of a Christian Hedonist*, rev. ed., 2014, accessed 12 November 2018, www.desiringgod.org/.../gods-covenant-with-david.html.

covenants he made and his commitment to preserving a remnant, as we saw in earlier chapters. So let us consider what God's covenants reveal about his character, and what this means for our characters. Given that the focus of this book is on remnant theology, we will orient this discussion specifically to the concerns of majorities, minorities and remnants.

Covenants and Hope

God's covenants with different generations of his people are a source of enormous hope. For example, it is because he knows God's covenants that the psalmist can say, "For the LORD is good and his love endures forever; his faithfulness continues through all generations" (Ps 100:5). In his prayerful reflections on the Psalms, Yohanna Katanacho, a Palestinian Christian, puts it succinctly: "When I consider the experience of Moses, Isaiah, and Asaph, I recognize that you are indeed the Holy Father who is full of goodness. You are the fountain of mercy and the mother who gave birth to compassion."[2] When we carefully consider the experience of the people of God in the Scriptures, we cannot help but realize that we are alive because we have received God's mercy and found God's grace.

God's covenants are an embodiment of God's goodness, love and faithfulness to all of his creation, particularly the human race. So, whenever we are tempted to wonder whether we in Africa can rely on God's covenants, we need to remember that he entered into a covenant of steadfast love with his creation before the foundation of the world. His covenants with Adam and Noah were never abrogated. He still cares for the world he has created, and over and over again in the Bible we read of a small number of people who were saved through the incomparably great protective power of a covenant-keeping God.

We do not enter into a covenant relationship knowing that it will fail. A covenant relies on and builds up relationships that are firmly rooted and trustworthy. We humans may have proved less than reliable covenant partners, but God is not unreliable. He is the one who ensures that the human parties to the covenant continue to exist so that his covenants still stand. This is why the remnant motif is an intrinsic part of the biblical narrative of God's covenant relationships with his creation.

God's commitment to his covenant of love is why we can offer hope to survivors of trauma and oppressed minorities. As was said before, their survival

---

2. Yohanna Katanacho, *Praying Through the Psalms* (Carlisle, UK: Langham Global Library, 2018), 145.

is not an accident. They were saved by the power of God and they can trust in the character of God. He is not cruel and vindictive but is eager to draw his people back into a relationship with himself. Even though Israel had ignored countless warnings and had turned her back on God, his rejection of the nation was not absolute. The survival of a remnant reveals the mystery of God's generous and gracious patience with his rebellious human race.

Why does God show this patience? The answer is seen in Nehemiah's prayer and in the words of Deuteronomy 4:31: "The LORD your God is a merciful God; he will not abandon or destroy you or forget the covenant with your ancestors, which he confirmed to them by oath." God is merciful and compassionate. He loves people, the crown of his creation, and so he chooses to bless them. But it is also because of his love for them that God punishes those who refuse to listen to him. He reduces some to the level of a remnant to allow them the opportunity to return to him, to the Lord their God, and to obey his commands. He reduces them to a remnant so that they can contemplate his mercies and then praise him. The remnant narrative is an extraordinary way of reminding of the richness of God's grace. The remnant story draws our attention to the fact that God is the greatest hero in kindness, a true legend in love, and the fountain of all positive and healthy virtues.

Covenants and Conduct

The biblical history of sin, punishment, forgiveness, and restoration reflects the unfolding of God's covenant and his desire to save his people and shape them to become like him. That is why it is important to remember the law that was revealed at the time when God entered into a covenant with Moses and the people of Israel at Sinai. And the law is based on God's character:

> It takes its shape from God's character as revealed in God's action. God cares for the needy, delivers the weak and the oppressed, acts with mercy and forgiveness and righteousness and justice, and is faithful; therefore, in the covenant relationship with God, we are to care for the needy, deliver the oppressed and act with mercy, forgiveness, righteousness, justice, and faithfulness.[3]

Read those words again, carefully. They are eye-opening in their focus on the link between God's covenant and God's character.

---

3. Birch, *Let Justice Roll Down*, quoted in Stassen and Gushee, *Kingdom Ethics*, 293.

Given that God's character does not change, the moral requirements of his covenants apply to all. This is true not only of the explicitly universal covenants with Adam and Noah but also of the Sinai covenant with the people of Israel. That covenant included the law that spelled out the relationships that should exist among individual Israelites, among all the tribes of God's chosen people, and between them and the surrounding nations.

When the Israelites were about to enter the promised land, they were preceded by the priests carrying the ark of the covenant, the symbol of God's covenant relationship with his people. Before setting out, Joshua gave a speech to the expectant people in which he spoke of "the ark of the covenant of the Lord of all the earth" (Josh 3:11). If God is indeed "the Lord of all the earth," then the covenants that signify his faithful and enduring presence offer the hope of righteousness and security for all of God's creation.

God's covenant laws do not apply only to a subset of humanity. The same moral and ethical requirements apply to everyone. No one is above anyone else, regardless of their social status or ethnic group. Deuteronomy 17:14–20 explicitly states that "the king is not to consider himself above his fellows, nor above the law. On the contrary, he is to be exemplary in paying heed to the law and obeying it. The king was not to be a super-Israelite, but a model Israelite."[4] God expects both leaders and followers to seek him as their Lord, creator, saviour, redeemer and sustainer. He is the one from whom they came and through whom they exist and for whom they exist. All are meant to live daily for his glory, honour and praise.

As those who follow God, we should seek to ensure that the social dynamic proclaimed in God's law is reflected in the social relations between majority and minority ethnic groups in Africa.

Covenants and Confidence

As we read about the various covenants God made with his people, it is striking how often these covenants are made with people whom their neighbours would have judged either unimportant or "different." They were not people of status in the world. Noah was probably mocked by his compatriots for building an ark on dry land. Abraham was a nomad, living far from the urban world of Ur where his extended family resided. He was an outsider in the land where God spoke to him. As shepherds, the Hebrew people were "detestable to the Egyptians" (Gen 46:34) when they first moved to Egypt. They had become

---

4. Wright, *Knowing God*, 81–82.

exploited slaves by the time Moses was born. The Egyptian majority would have ridiculed any suggestion that the Hebrew minority were the covenant people of God. David was the youngest brother, so insignificant that he was not even summoned to join the rest of the family when the prophet Samuel asked to meet with them. His royal descendants would have been regarded as minor kings by the great kings of Egypt and Assyria and Babylon. Even Jesus, who offered himself in the new covenant, was born in humble circumstances in a minor nation rather than into one of great nations like Greece or Rome that dominated the world in his day.

None of God's covenants were made with "majorities" – unless we count Adam and Eve and Noah as such because they were the sole representatives of the human race in their day.

It is also important to note that many of these people were "remnants." Noah and his family were the sole survivors when God destroyed the world in the flood. Years after God scattered the nations at Babel, he selected a single man, Abraham, as a "remnant" to become the father of the nation that would make God known to the world. Moses was an abandoned baby, and when he grew to adulthood he had to flee alone into the wilderness to escape prosecution. David and his descendants had to fight for survival against other stronger nations. The Jewish nation into which Jesus was born had grown from a remnant who straggled back to the promised land after the exile in Babylon and had later survived the terrors of the reign of Antiochus Epiphanes and the Maccabean wars before being conquered by Rome.

Clearly there is no shame in being a minority or a remnant. God repeatedly chose minorities to bear his message to the nations and to be his representatives of earth. So those of us who are minorities are not obliged to sit back in silence while majorities speak over our heads. We can speak out with confidence, knowing that in the past God has spoken through minorities, and there is no reason why he cannot do so again.

We do not have to be powerful for God to work through us. All we need to do is rely on God. This need to rely on God is established over and over again in Scripture. Gideon, for example, had to work with only a remnant of his once large army in order to show that his victory would come through the power of God. God reduced their number from 32,000 to three hundred so that neither Gideon nor any of his soldiers could take credit for the victory over the Midianites. The glory was due to God alone (Judg 7). In the same way, God can save a remnant and bless the world through them, even though they seem to be a people without political, social, or economic power.

The recurring motif of "the few" suggests that we can apply the concept of a remnant in all generations of God's people. Through his grace, mercy, love, and compassion, he always spares a few people whom he will eventually bless and multiply to fulfil his covenantal promises. The fact that a remnant was saved reminds us of God's graciousness and underscores the doctrine of grace. So does the truth that the saved remnant becomes a saving remnant. The remnant survives and is saved as it seeks to protect others.

Covenants and Concern

A recurring feature of the covenants God made with Israel's patriarchs is that people do not keep their part of the contract. This was one of the primary reasons why the chosen people of God lost their God-promised land and freedom:

> The people of Judah and those who live in Jerusalem . . . have returned to the sins of their ancestors, who refused to listen to my words. They have followed other gods to serve them. Both Israel and Judah have broken the covenant I made with their ancestors. Therefore, this is what the LORD says: "I will bring on them a disaster they cannot escape." (Jer 11:9–11)

Other prophets, great and small, also spoke of the disastrous consequences of breaking God's covenant: "Sound the alarm. The enemy descends like an eagle on the people of the Lord for they have broken my covenant and revolted against my law" (Hos 8:1 NLT).

Being in a covenant relationship with God was no guarantee of prosperity regardless of how one lived. God does not show favouritism. In fact, as God warned through Amos, "You only have I chosen of all the families of the earth; therefore I will punish you for all your sins" (Amos 3:2). We should heed this warning. So should all majorities, who assume that because God has blessed them with numbers and prosperity, they will automatically continue to enjoy these things.

We who are members of God's church and who share in the blessings of God's covenants should also live with the awareness that we too will be subject to his judgement if we do not obey his word and live in a way that reflects God's character. This concern should not destroy our hope, but it should prevent us from excessive self-confidence. It is God who judges and God who delivers. Our calling is to be faithful in loving God and others.

6

The Reality of a Divided Humanity

God's covenants were made with nations and with individuals, for in God's economy human beings matter. Jesus's parable of leaving the ninety-nine sheep to look for the one lost sheep vividly illustrates how much God values the individual, the minority, the remnant. But we do not share God's perspective. We rarely think of ourselves or others as God's creation. Instead, we look at others through the lens of our ethnic, social, political, economic or religious affiliations. Consequently, human dignity and human life are not valued. The categorization of African society into majority and minority ethnic groups distorts our concept of human value and our interconnectedness. The marginalized and disinherited find the earth inhospitable, while those in majority groups cling to power.

The nineteenth-century author James Hunt provides a good illustration of someone who categorized others in a way that granted the categorizer, or the colonizer, full rights and denied the rights of others. He "categorized humanity as civilised, barbarous and savage in dealing with recognition under international law. For him, full recognition belonged to civilised nations of *right*, while savages and barbarians had limited or no entitlement to recognition."[1]

Today few would be as public as he was about their categorization of others, but such categorization still continues. We see it when an American president

---

1. Kajit J. Bagu, *Constitutionalism and the Global South* (Oxford: Routledge, 2020), 78, quoting James Hunt's 1863 paper on "the Negro's place in nature."

refers to "shithole countries"[2] and we also see it in how we in Africa treat the minorities within our own countries.

I have been involved in just peace-making in Nigeria and elsewhere for many years now, and have spent much of this time trying to dig down into the root causes of human hostility. Why is it that human interactions and relationships are so often defined by discrimination, rejection, hatred, conflict and violence? Why do minorities so often experience oppression, rejection, destruction and death? I have come to realize that the issues involved are very elusive but also very pervasive. In this chapter, we will look at the broad role of sin and judgement in these divisions, and in the next we will consider the role of assumptions that stem from our inner insecurity and from our fear of being vulnerable.

Divisions and Sin

Humans have been on this road of discrimination and dehumanization since the fall of Adam and Eve. In fact it could be said that the social crises that cause humans to pit themselves against each other, to create dividing walls, or to build fences that separate them from each other are re-enactments of the narrative of Genesis 3. Adam and Eve turned their back on God and sought to be like God, thereby bringing sin into the world. Similarly, it is our worship of self-made gods – the idols of pride, tribalism, ethnicity, religion, politics, money, sex and power – that brings suffering and encourages our greed, jealousy, hatred, exclusion, scapegoating and stereotyping. Advances in theology, art, science and technology have done little to reverse the trend.

Thus the social and moral situations in which we find ourselves in Africa are not simply the result of religion, politics, or anything else we may want to blame. These situations reveal the idolatry and other moral sins that turn us against each other and against the environment in which we live.

It is important, however, to recognize that while divisions within families, between groups, and between majorities and minorities are undoubtedly caused by sin, they are also part of God's judgement on sin.

---

2. NBC News, "Trump Refers to Haiti and African Nations as 'Shithole Countries,'" https://www.nbcnews.com/politics/white-house/trump-referred-haiti-african-countries-shithole-nations-n836946.

Divisions and Judgement

God can use division and discrimination as instruments of judgement when people break their covenant relationship with him. We should not doubt the reality of his judgement, for the events of the fall provide insights into the reality of sin and death. The plain truth is that disobedience to God's revealed will and disregard for his covenant relationship with us will always bring his judgement upon us, and these judgements may divide us.

We see this clearly in the events of Genesis 11, when people decided to build a civilization that excluded God:

> At one time all the people of the world spoke one language and used the same words. As the people migrated to the east, they found a plain in the land of Babylonia and settled there. They began saying to each other, "Let's make bricks and harden them with fire." (In this region bricks were used instead of stone, and tar was used for mortar.) Then they said, "Come, let's build a great city for ourselves with a tower which reaches into the sky. This will make us famous and keep us from being scattered all over the world." (Gen 11:1–4 NLT)

God immediately passed judgement on this pride by confusing their language and disorganizing their unhealthy oneness by scattering them across the face of the earth:

> But the LORD came down to look at the city and the tower the people were building. "Look!" he said. "The people are united, and they all speak the same language. After this, nothing they set out to do will be impossible for them! Come, let's go down and confuse the people with different languages. Then they won't be able to understand each other." In that way, the LORD scattered them all over the world, and they stopped building the city. (Gen 11:5–8 NLT)

There are other instances in the Bible where we also see that division is God's judgement upon human sin, pride, and disobedience. For example, King Solomon took foreign wives and allowed them to turn him away from worshipping and obeying God. As a result, after his death, the nation of Israel which had been experiencing social, economic and political harmony, was suddenly faced with sharp conflict and was divided into the Northern and Southern Kingdoms. When Rehoboam, the first king of the southern kingdom of Judah, wanted to go to war in order to unite the nation, God would not allow him to do so, saying "for this is my doing" (2 Chr 11:1–4). The division of the nation was God's judgement on Solomon's lack of fidelity to the Davidic covenant. Today, too, our divisions reveal God's displeasure because we have broken his covenant of steadfast love and grace.

Despair Is Not an Option

Some will see this chapter as profoundly discouraging. If humans are sinful, and will always be in conflict and divided, what is the point of trying to live uprightly and trying to foster unity and heal divisions? They will continue to exist whatever we do.

That argument has a touch of truth – we will never ultimately solve the sin problem on our own, and only God's mercy can restrain his judgement. But the whole of Scripture teaches us that God does not want us to abandon hope and give up any attempt to live in the way he desires. He gave the people of his Israel his laws to guide them in creating a just society, and spoke through his prophets to make it clear that inequitable divisions of any kind must be addressed because they are not part of God's ultimate will for the human race. He created us to live in community with him, with one another, and with the environment. He created us to bear his image, and so to be characterized by unity, love, justice, compassion and mercy, and he expects us to pursue these things, even if we cannot fully achieve them.

Others may argue that if divisions are God's instrument of judgement, then minority groups deserve their suffering. They are being punished by God for the evils of their ancestors. So if we try to correct injustices and raise the statues of minorities, we are opposing God's plan.

Any such argument is deeply flawed. First, it ignores the fact that, as was shown in the chapter on covenants, God entered into his covenants with minorities and chose to bless them. Second, this argument assumes that we know exactly what God is doing. But we do not know his plans. He made this very clear to this people, "As the heavens are higher than the earth, so are my ways higher than your ways and my thoughts than your thoughts" (Isa 55:9). Third, it ignores the Old Testament prophets' repeated calls for justice for the poor and the oppressed. Finally, it ignores God's character of love and mercy, which led him to declare, "Only if the heavens above can be measured and the foundations of the earth below be searched out will I reject all the descendants of Israel because of all they have done" (Jer 31:37). Because of his covenant love, God does not reject even those he disciplines. We are not called to be stricter than God!

As we reflect on what this chapter means for this generation of African believers in Christ, some of us will have to hear it as a call to repentance for our own sins that have caused divisions, or for our tolerance of injustice to others. But for others, and especially for minorities, this chapter may be a call to take heart. God does not ignore sin, and he demands justice. We can bring our cause before him and before his people knowing that God is both just and merciful. He cares about those who suffer and he calls on his people to do something to alleviate their suffering.

7

Remnants, Assumptions and Injustice

In the previous chapter, we saw how sin and God's judgement affect our actions. But it is not enough just to say that; we also need to understand the mechanisms through which sin works in our world and why we think and act as we do. It will not be long before we realize that often our world is ruled by assumptions. The *Longman Dictionary of Contemporary English* defines an assumption as "a thing that is accepted as true . . . without proof."[1] Daily, we are inundated with assumptions. Some of them are necessary: When I board a bus and my fellow passengers say that the bus is going to Abuja, I believe them, although I have no proof that what they say is correct until the bus turns onto the highway to Abuja. Sometimes we need to operate on the basis of assumptions – but when our assumptions are wrong, the consequences are dire.

Assumptions do not only operate on the individual level, but also on the societal level. Many of the social, political and economic policies our societies have adopted are largely based on assumptions. Too often, so are our laws and the judgements that result from them. There is a sense in which these assumptions can be said to reveal the influence of the master of lies, for they cause humans to tell huge lies and to believe them to be true. The public policies we implement and the political and moral core values that we hold may be false.

Acknowledging that truth may threaten to shatter our whole idea of reality. We prefer to cling to assumptions that make us feel that we are superior. Like nineteenth-century Westerners, we want to be able to categorize people neatly as civilized, barbarians and savages. Our terminology is different: today we use categories such as majority and minority, developed economy versus

---

1. *Longman Dictionary of Contemporary English* (Essex, UK: Longman Group UK, 1987), 54.

developing economy, and so on. Too often, such labelling distorts our grasp of our shared humanity.

Assumptions Have Consequences

The consequences of assumptions can be enormous. The apostle Paul would not have been the first or the last to die at the hands of a mob who made assumptions about his behaviour (Acts 21:29). They assumed that he had committed sacrilege by bringing Gentiles into the heart of the temple. The commander of the troops stationed near the temple who intervened and arrested Paul assumed he was an Egyptian troublemaker who had recently stirred up a revolt and led four thousand terrorists out into the wilderness (Acts 21:38). He was amazed to learn that Paul was actually a Roman citizen and entitled to the legal protections given to Roman citizens.

At Paul's trial after this arrest, the Jewish authorities acted on a different assumption, not an assumption about a person but an assumption about ethics. They assumed that the end justifies the means. They were determined to prevent Paul from preaching the gospel, and so they falsely accused him of being a "troublemaker" and a "ringleader" who stirred up riots (Acts 24:5). Their accusations were baseless, but because they feared the spread of Christianity and wanted to stop it, they felt free to assume that Paul's intentions were evil and that their own motives were pure. We may recognize similar assumptions at work today.

Paul's trial was by no means the last time that assumptions have disrupted the work of the church, and sometimes these assumptions are made by Christians about their fellow Christians. Even those with little knowledge of Western history know that there were times when Christians in Europe made assumptions about their Jewish neighbours and massacred them. They were also times when Christians persecuted their Christian brothers and sisters because they assumed that they were heretics. Christian leaders assumed that believers with a radical and passionate commitment to Christ posed a threat to the religious hierarchy and mobilized unsuspecting members of the Christian community to lynch them.

But we should look further than the simple equation of assumptions and mob action. That is an easy target. But the effect of assumptions can be even more insidious and harmful when they are part of a world view. It may be helpful to first look at an example of this through the eyes of someone who is not African, so that we can turn back to Africa with clearer vision. So I will begin with the teachings of the famous Greek philosopher, Plato. Plato's teaching was in accord with the biblical account of creation in Genesis in that he recognized that human beings have both a body and a soul (spirit), with the body frequently understood as the material part of a human being and the soul (spirit) as the immaterial element of a person. In Scripture, these two aspects of a person are clearly intrinsically connected.

But Plato operated on the assumption that the material is vastly inferior to the spiritual. In fact, he regarded the material body as evil and thought that only the soul or spirit is good. This dualism suggested that the body and soul were fundamentally incompatible. The body was seen as no more than "an evil container for the pure soul. For the Greek, salvation ultimately meant redemption from the body when the soul is finally released from the prison-house of the flesh."[2] This is the opposite of the biblical view, represented by God's statement in Genesis that the physical world he had created, and the human beings in it, were all "very good" (Gen 1:31).

You may think that Plato's belief that the body is evil is a minor point, but when this belief became so accepted that it was an assumption shared by many, it had major consequences. Because the body and soul, the two aspects of a human being, were assumed to be utterly separate, the belief grew that what happened to the one part did not affect the other. People started to believe that what they did with their bodies would have no effect on their souls (spirits), with disastrous consequences for ethics and morality:

> The Platonic view makes us believe that we can sin without sin affecting our spirit. It also makes salvation stop at the point of delivering us from the body, the evil container of the soul. It undercuts the biblical account of God's creation of humans as "very good" and without any inherent evil in its physical substance. These assumptions fail to help us realize that though the body was created good, with the fall of Adam and Eve, the body now suffers from moral corruption just like the soul.[3]

A careful reading of the Scriptures reveals, however, that this thinking was based on a false premise. If Christ himself "became flesh and made his dwelling among us" (John 1:14), how can "flesh" (the body) be evil? Nor was Christ's body merely a concession to living in an evil world, for the resurrected Christ had a resurrected body. It was different from the disciples' bodies in

---

2. "Human Beings as Body and Soul," *Reformation Study Bible, ESV* (Orlando, FL: Reformation Trust, 2015), 1948.

3. "Human Beings as Body and Soul," 1948.

some respects, but it was still a physical body for the resurrected Christ could be touched by the disciples and ate meals with them. No wonder that Paul stressed that there is redemption for both our bodies and our souls (Rom 8:23).

Plato's assumption was wrong. Yet this Platonic dualism became a cornerstone of Western civilisation and Western Christianity was deeply influenced by this assumed division between sacred and secular, with harmful effects that endure to this day and even affect Africa. There are still many African Christians who see their faith as purely a spiritual matter that does not affect the details of their daily lives.

We see another example of a dangerous assumption in Europe in the seventeen and eighteenth centuries. This era has become known as the Age of Enlightenment. It was a time when many people in the West assumed that they had "come of age" and no longer needed God, the Bible or Christian tradition. It was assumed that science and technology would do away with all conflicts, violence, hunger, drought, diseases, epidemics and plagues, and so on. T. M. Kitwood put it like this:

> The general intellectual mood in Europe was one of self-congratulation. Through enlightenment, it seemed that peace, virtue, and humanity were steadily replacing the barbarism of former ages. Science was bringing more and more insight into the natural world.[4]

The Enlightenment deceived the West, and eventually the entire globe. Humans dreamed of creating a world where perfect peace and endless happiness were guaranteed. It was claimed that humankind would enjoy true social, economic and political unity, harmony, and cohesion. But it was not long before the First World War shattered these illusions and proved their assumptions were faulty.

Assumptions also contributed to the Second World War. As Hitler rose to power in Germany, he was supported by German Christians who assumed that Germany needed a strong person like Hitler to rebuild it after the Great Depression (1929–1939). They also assumed that they could believe Hitler when he said that Christians were the "most important factor safeguarding our national heritage."[5]

Accepting those assumptions opened the door for German Christians to believe other even more damaging assumptions. They did not challenge Hitler's

---

4. T. M. Kitwood, *What Is Human?* (London: Inter-Varsity Press, 1970), 55.

5. Eberhard Bethge, *Dietrich Bonhoeffer: A Biography*, rev. ed. (Minneapolis: Fortress, 2000), 262, cited in Stassen and Gushee, *Kingdom*, 125.

belief that patriotic Germans were morally obliged to protect the "blue-eyed, blond-haired people of Nordic stock, or 'Aryans.'" They accepted that Hitler had "the right to declare who was worthy of life and who was not, who was to be maimed by sterilization or experimented upon in the interest of attaining racial purity, and who was to be used as slave labour to further the Nazi empire."[6] They did not object when Hitler called for "the 'racial purity' of the civil service and eventually of the church". This policy meant that "no Christian of Jewish descent would be permitted to hold a position in the church."[7]

These policies favoured the majority, who were German Christians, and harmed minorities. But because their eyes were blinkered by their previous assumptions, many Christians did not see anything wrong with such inhumane policies. They assumed that because Hitler spoke about the need for Christian morality and referred to divine providence they could support his actions. Stassen and Gushee explain that "Christians were flattered by Hitler's claim to support Christianity, and they lacked the biblical commitment to standards of justice that would have warned them against unjust plans."[8] The German theologians and ethicists Dietrich Bonhoeffer and Karl Barth were among the few Christians who risked their lives to speak out against the forces of evil that were working in and against the church.

German Christians' unquestioning acceptance of the assumptions of Hitler ultimately caused the death of six million Jews and five million other minorities. Whole communities were wiped out – starving and dying as forced labour in mines and industries or simply executed on the spot or sent to the gas chambers. And it was not only these minorities who died – thousands of others from around the world died when Hitler's aggression led to the Second World War.

Assumptions in Africa

It is easy for us to point fingers at the German Christians under Hitler and wonder why they were so blind. But we in Africa also act on the basis of unfounded assumptions. If you doubt this, read what Dr. Samuel Kunhiyop has to say about his experience with accusations of witchcraft. He has learned

---

6. Friedman, "The Other Victims of the Nazis," in *Social Education* 59, no. 6 (October 1995): 339–41.

7. Stassen and Gushee, *Kingdom Ethics*, 126.

8. Stassen and Gushee, 127.

that there are still so-called Christians across Africa who kill those whom they assume are witches or wizards.[9] Some of those accused are very young children!

Meanwhile there are others who assume that Christians from minority ethnic groups are not qualified to be leaders in the church. They assume that to allow people from minority ethnic groups to have access to spiritual leadership is wrong. In fact, they tend to accept the truism that it is the birth right of the majority to rule, while those from the minority who help them to maintain the status quo must be the servants and slaves of the majority group. Those from minority groups therefore cannot use their gifts to serve the church.

On the political front, too, African democratic systems are riddled with assumptions which mean that the systems do not work for the benefit of all. Majority tribes assume that they do not need to share power with the minority groups. Political office holders or elites assume that laws are not meant for them. They assume that the rules are meant for the poor masses, not for those who are in power. As a result the rule of law is unfairly implemented.

Instead of enjoying our diversity and plurality and harnessing our God-given gifting for the common good, we have erected barriers that estrange us from each other. This has been very detrimental to the development of the African continent, for no society can truly develop when so-called minority ethnic groups (or minority nationalities) are denied the opportunity to participate fully in all aspects of the life of their motherland.

Conclusion

Assumptions are like the COVID-19 virus. Many who are infected do not know they are infected, and unwittingly spread the disease. But when the virus manifests itself, its effects can be dire. Many of those who do not die of it are left with impaired health and may take months to return to full health and vitality. Meanwhile the whole society suffers and relationships are fractured by our fear of this virus. In the same way, our assumptions about each other destroy relationships, maim lives, and cripple our societies.

As I write this, scientists are racing to develop vaccines to build our immunity to the COVID-19 virus. But how do we develop an immunity to the assumptions virus? What can we as African Christians do to free our beloved continent from the harm it causes? That is the topic of our next chapter.

---

9. Samuel Waje Kunhiyop, *Witchcraft Belief and Accusations; A Biblical and Christian Perspective* (Jos: Challenge Press, 2019), 22–23.

8

Facing Our Wrong Assumptions

In the previous chapter, I described assumptions as being like the COVID-19 virus. They spread rapidly and lurk out of sight in apparently healthy people, like you and me. But these "healthy" people can spread the COVID-19 virus, infecting others and causing the deaths of vulnerable people. This assumes the virus lurks in all of us, majorities and minorities. If you doubt this, see how you respond to the following assumptions.

We Are Different

Majority groups tend to see themselves as superior to the minorities we have been talking about as remnants in this book. But if you have been paying attention as you read, you will have noticed that one of the implications of covenant theology is that we are all a remnant. Why? Because, given the many diseases and disasters that have come upon this world as a whole and on Africa in our case, the odds against your ever having come into existence are very high. The historical odds against your ethnic group having survived are also very high. The sole reason that you exist today is because your ancestors survived by the grace of God. So in that sense, a majority is no different from a minority.

Secondly, because of our shared status as beings made in the image of God (Gen 1:27), we are all equal in his sight. This is a truth that we are all happy to acknowledge when it benefits us, and that we are equally happy to overlook when it benefits someone else, especially if that person is from a minority group. We assume that we deserve what God has given us, and that they do not. Such thinking can even affect minorities who accept a system that declares them inferior and then seek out some other group that they too can look down on.

Often, this assumption is never put into words; it may not even be acknowledged in our conscious thinking, but it lies close to the surface and affects our actions in relation to each other. It prevents us from living by the Golden Rule: "So in everything, do to others what you would have them do to you" (Matt 7:12).

There Is Not Enough to Go Round

Our cat recently produced three very lively kittens. Today, it seems that she wanted a rest, and so she brought them a rat to eat and went off to a cool place and fell asleep. She assumed that the rat would keep them occupied and that they would all share in the meal, for it was a large rat.

But the kittens had a different set of assumptions. The biggest and strongest kitten chased its siblings away and kept half the rat for itself. These kittens had the same mother. They were born on the same day. They were growing up and playing together. Yet, because one of them happened to have the advantage of weight and size, it assumed that it was entitled to seize as much as it could for itself in case there was not enough for each one of them.

I realized that the kitten was mirroring the human world, where the principle of the survival of the fittest plays out. The kitten was perfectly illustrating the fear of vulnerability. It assumed that there would not be enough rat for all of them, and so it created a scarcity for the other kittens where there had been none. It assumed that what was enough would be insufficient. Assumptions like this made it selfish, just as they make us selfish. We hoard what was meant to be shared.

Yet, despite our hoarding, we still cannot find fulfilment. Instead we feel extremely vulnerable and experience enormous anxiety and agitation. We then begin to operate on the basis of scarcity, which Brené Brown calls, "the never-enough problem." This means that we think of ourselves as "never perfect enough, never powerful enough, never successful enough, never smart enough, never certain enough, never extraordinary enough." She concludes that "We get scarcity because we live it."[1] This is very true!

The assumption of scarcity means that majority groups are unwilling to share resources with minority groups. These resources may be tangible, like farmland and other natural resources, or they may be intangible resources like access to power and positions of leadership. Leaders from different groups are

---

1. Brené Brown, *Daring Greatly: How the Courage to Be Vulnerable Transforms the Way We Live, Love, Parent and Lead* (New York: Penguin, 2012), 24–25.

locked in power struggles because they think that only if they are in control will their people get the resources they need. Sadly, this has often been true in Africa, where politicians (and sadly even some church leaders) practise nepotism and incite ethnic rivalry. But God is the one who provides enough for all he has made – if they are willing to share it. Think of how different the circumstances of Nigeria would be if its vast oil wealth was used for the common good, rather than for the enrichment of a few and the impoverishment of others whose lives are destroyed by the environmental and social impact of the oil industry. Similar situations exist in many countries in Africa where resources that could be used to bless all groups are hoarded by a few.

When we are tempted to claim resources for ourselves rather than sharing them, we need to be reminded of Jesus's words: "No one can serve two masters. Either you will hate the one and love the other, or you will be devoted to the one and despise the other. You cannot serve both God and money" (Matt 6:24).

I Am in Charge

Because we do not want to risk vulnerability, we like to assume that we are in charge of our own destiny and circumstances. This assumption is particularly prevalent in the West, where innumerable self-help books encourage people to "take control of your life." Such books are also circulating widely in Africa.

In Africa, however, the options for taking charge of one's life are sometimes different from those promoted in the West. Africans do not think purely in material terms when they hear this phrase, for they know the reality of the spirit world and its influence in the material world. For many in Africa, the way to be in charge of their life is to enlist the services of the spirits by acquiring charms, amulets, ointments and other ritual objects from traditional witch doctors. Some will go to great lengths to obtain an object that they assume will give them power and protection and enable them to be in charge of their destiny.

Christian believers are not immune to this desire, and there are Christian preachers who peddle holy handkerchiefs and holy water and the like to give people a sense of protection and control. Some Christians even use a Bible as a kind of amulet, believing that if they have a Bible close at hand, they will be protected from physical and spiritual danger.

In the context of this book, there are two problems with such practices. One is that we forget that God is ultimately in control of the world. No charm or amulet can thwart his plans. Nor can the accumulation of wealth, as Jesus reminded us in his parable about the rich man who said to himself, "You have plenty of grain laid up for many years. Take life easy; eat, drink and be merry."

He thought he was in charge of his own life. "But God said to him, 'You fool! This very night your life will be demanded from you. Then who will get what you have prepared for yourself?'" (Luke 12:19–20).

The second problem, and the key one in this book, is that when we assume that we are in charge, we assume that we can do what we want – "eat, drink and be merry" – without regard to the needs of others. Majorities who live in comfort may not even notice the suffering of minorities, just as Lazarus did not notice the suffering of the poor man at his gate (Luke 16:19–21). But God does see the suffering, and he notes our lack of concern. This point too was driven home by Jesus when he told the parable of the sheep and the goats, ending with the stern warning that "whatever you did not do for one of the least of these, you did not do for me" (Matt 25:45).

Minorities, who are disillusioned and disheartened by their constant struggle for recognition can, however, take heart from the fact that God is in charge. He will uphold their just cause and will judge those who abuse them.

I Am a Winner Not a Loser

When we are overpowered by suppositions and assumptions, we fail to grasp that God has blessed others with potential. Our assumptions eclipse our Christian moral vision and perspective. We cannot see the dignity of our fellow men and women, nor can we see ourselves as we really are. Our vision becomes distorted. When we forget the truth and jump to conclusions, we do tremendous evil. We look for scapegoats who can carry the blame if something goes wrong. In this way we avoid the need to feel vulnerable. Our arrogance fuels a competitive spirit.

I did not realize how much I too am a servant of (or, in fact, a slave to) this competitive spirit until the coronavirus epidemic hit Nigeria, and we went into lockdown. Our church could no longer meet together, and so it was decided that we should form small worship cells. On the first Sunday I attended one of the worship cells close to my home. On the second Sunday, as was our custom, the leader of the worship cell announced the amount that had been donated in offerings the previous Sunday. He then went on to compare what our worship cell had given with the giving of the other worship cells, announcing that we had given the most. I felt extremely happy and proud. But when the pastor stood up to preach, he mistakenly announced that we had come second in our giving. Although he was quickly corrected by an elder, we were momentarily shocked. Immediately the truth was revealed, everybody perked up, proud of what the group had done.

Suddenly I saw the danger of a competitive spirit. We were no longer willing to see ourselves as a part of the church as a whole. We enjoyed being better than the others. Pride overtook us. We were happy that we were in the winning party. We assumed that our giving more meant that we were different from our fellow church members. We began to look down on them.

That is exactly the way hypocrisy begins, and it is utterly at variance with the mind of Christ, who washed his disciples' feet (John 13:1–14) and told us that "the greatest among you will be your servant. For those who exalt themselves will be humbled, and those who humble themselves will be exalted" (Matt 23:11–12).

9

The Way Ahead

Every year I try to read through the Bible, and therefore I have been reading the following verse year after year:

> Remember those in prison, as if you were there yourself. Remember also those being mistreated, as if you felt their pain in your own bodies. (Heb 13:3 NLT)

Perhaps you know that verse too? Perhaps you have taken it seriously and put it into practice?

It has only recently occurred to me that this verse could also apply to those minority ethnic groups in Africa who are mistreated by their brothers and sisters from so-called majority ethnic groups. Sometimes we have to face hard truths when we begin to take passages like this seriously! Often we begin praying comfortably in our homes and churches for a specific need, but then God starts to work his purposes. Suddenly we discover that we cannot just pray for those who are suffering; we are also being called upon to act on their behalf.

This is what led to the writing of this book, but this cannot be the end of the matter. There is a greater work to be done, a work that involves all God's people whether they belong to majority or to minority ethnic groups. Let us prayerfully consider God's way ahead.

Following in the Footsteps of Jesus

God's covenants with Adam and with Noah include all of us in Africa. After all, everyone alive today is a direct descendant first of Adam and then of Noah, whose family was the only one to survive the flood. As we saw in chapter 4, God emphasizes over and over again in his covenant undertaking to Noah that the covenant was established between him and every "living creature" (Gen 9:8–17). This is why both God's friends and God's enemies enjoy the seasons.

Jesus reminds us of this in his Sermon on the Mount when he says that "your Father in heaven . . . causes his sun to rise on the evil and the good, and sends rain on the righteous and the unrighteous" (Matt 5:45; see also Gen 8:22). God provides for all humanity, for both ethnic majorities and ethnic minorities. He does not discriminate against or marginalize any member of his creation.

In many ways, Matthew 5:43–48 is a summary of the great Sermon on the Mount in which Jesus reveals much about the relationship between the Old Testament passages his listeners knew so well and his kingdom. Throughout the sermon, Jesus shows that his words are fundamental to the way of life to which his followers are called and through which God will be glorified. This means that we too, as his followers, are to love our neighbours because God loves his creation and because we, his children, are called to be like him.

Jesus also explains what it actually means to love others. It is easy for all of us to love people who are like us, who come from our own group. We understand how they think, and they understand us. There is nothing special about such love – it is no more than everyone else is doing. But the love Jesus wants us to show is much more challenging: We are to love our enemies, to love those who are different, to love those who sometimes make us feel uncomfortable, to love those who belong to other groups in our society, regardless of the status of those groups. This is not an optional extra. This is Jesus's new commandment, one he repeats in John 13:34: "A new command I give you: Love one another. As I have loved you, so you must love one another."

Jesus is not happy with half-hearted love for those in other groups. He tells us to strive to be "perfect." Eugene Peterson's paraphrase in *The Message* translation vividly captures the sense of what he is saying:

> In a word, what I'm saying is, *Grow up.* You're kingdom subjects.
> Now live like it. Live out your God-created identity. Live generously
> and graciously toward others, the way God lives toward you.

But it is all very well to nod in agreement with all that has been said. The difficulty lies in the doing, in putting it into practice. What must we do as members of a majority group or as members of a minority?

Learning to Live and Love as Members of a Majority Group

We Africans like to remind the world of the African concept of *ubuntu*. There can be no doubt that the concept is a good one, but if we are honest we must sometimes admit that we apply it more in the context of people who are like us than we do people from other ethnic groups. It is time to expand our concern to include everyone in God's world. The actions we will have to take will differ from community to community and from individual to individual. But they must all begin in the same place: in prayer.

Adjusting Our Hearts and Minds

As we pray, reflecting on God's goodness as revealed in his covenants, we will find ourselves infused with a spirit of humility. And as we recognize our own sinfulness, we shall become aware that we cannot judge others. Our recognition of God's power and grace in dealing with our weaknesses should enable us to deal gently with others, even if we feel they are weaker than we are. If we truly grasp the importance of the remnant motif and allow it to shape us, our powers of discernment will be trained as we pray to distinguish good from evil, without regard for people's status. The apostle James reminds us that we must act without favouritism or partiality (Jas 2:9). God requires us to act with moral courage, carefulness, fair-mindedness, and honesty.

But, you may say, "I live in a multi-ethnic city and I don't discriminate on the basis of ethnicity at all." At one level that may be true, yet sometimes our discrimination may be subconscious. This is why we must devote ourselves to prayer (Col 4:2). Prayer will open us up to the gracious work of the Holy Spirit. This means that our praying needs to be ongoing.

Perhaps we can take a lesson from life in Africa. We all know the fearsome power of termites to destroy everything in their path. The only way to prevent damage to our property or possessions is to use treated wood and to inspect wooden structures regularly. Assumptions about others are like these termites as they can eat away at the heart of our society and our churches and can bring them crashing down in ruin. This means that we need to carry out inspections under God's searchlights. If we do not monitor our intentions and our actions through prayer, our attempts to build bridges between us and our neighbours will fail and we shall be cut off from one another by deep chasms even though we may meet and worship together.

One of Jesus's final prayers before his crucifixion was "that all of them may be one" (John 17:21). Barriers between his followers are "the devil's work" (1 John 3:8); however, as we allow the Holy Spirit to work in us, the areas which we need to confess and to allow him to change will become evident.

Let us hear what Paul wrote to the church at Ephesus. In this section of the letter, he is addressing Gentiles, members of the majority group in Ephesus:

> Remember that at that time you were separate from Christ,
> excluded from citizenship in Israel and foreigners to the covenants
> of the promise, without hope and without God in the world.

> But now in Christ Jesus, you who once were far away have been
> brought near by the blood of Christ. For he himself is our peace,
> who has made the two groups one and has destroyed the barrier,
> the dividing wall of hostility by setting aside in his flesh the law
> with its commands and regulations. His purpose was to create in
> himself one new humanity out of the two, thus making peace, and
> in one body to reconcile both of them to God through the cross,
> by which he put to death their hostility. (Eph 2:12–16)

God had brought the Jews and the Gentiles together in Jesus Christ, making
peace between them. Surely he can do the same for groups in Africa!

As we pray, we need to repent of any discrimination against others and
any demonization of other groups and acknowledge that all such behaviour
represents a turning aside from God's command to love one another.

Adjusting Our Attitudes and Actions

But it is not enough simply to be humble before God in prayer; we must also
allow this spirit of humility to manifest itself to others. This may not be easy.
Without God's grace, no amount of education can actually dislodge the fear of
allowing ourselves to be seen as mere people. It is hard to face up to the reality
of our vulnerability and of our need to depend on God's infinitely greater
power. Our self-interest drives us to dominate others and to keep for ourselves
the natural resources that God has graciously given to all. We may want to cling
to food, money and power, rather than to share these resources with our fellow
human beings from minority ethnic groups. The fear of becoming vulnerable,
above anything else, may prompt us to discriminate against our fellow humans.

But if some are assumed to be or regard themselves as superior, others
must be labelled as second-class citizens because they belong to a minority
ethnic group. Those of us who belong to a majority ethnic group, must therefore
think carefully. We have to act decisively against such indoctrination. Once
again the Scriptures show us how to do so. You may recall how Paul healed
a lame man in Lystra (Acts 14:8–18). When they observed the miracle, the
people of the town decided that "The gods have come down to us in human
form." Paul and Barnabas, we are told, "tore their clothes and rushed out into
the crowd, shouting . . .' 'We are only human like you.'" The apostles knew that
they did not deserve the respect being shown to them. Members of majority
ethnic groups are not gods to whom the minority citizens should bow down.
Like Paul and Barnabas we must make sure that those around us hear this truth.

There are large actions we may need to take to establish this truth, but there are also countless small ways in which we can do this each day. We may need to learn to wait humbly in the queue, to remember to say "please" and "thank you," to greet with a smile all who cross our paths no matter how we would categorize them . . . the list is endless. None of these actions is terribly demanding but, as we act, we are reminding ourselves and others that we are all the beloved children of the Most High God.

By consciously acting as Jesus would want us to do, we will be humbling ourselves and fighting the ethnic divisions that exist today as a result of human pride. Gradually we shall lose the desire to pit ourselves against others and we shall discover the blessings of cooperating for the common good.

Adjusting Our Churches and Communities

Sadly this lesson needs to be learned in the church as well. Too often, churches are divided along ethnic lines. And even churches whose members are a mix of various ethnicities sometimes act as if ethnic minorities are not as important as the majority ethnic group in God's eyes. We as the church have forgotten that God created each person – man or woman – in his image and likeness (Gen 1:27). Our worth does not depend on where we were born or the tribe or ethnic group we belong to. It has nothing to do with the size of our ethnic group. As members of his church, we are to be one in the Lord.

Too many African Christians have forgotten that life in the kingdom of God is supposed to be completely different from life in the old system which we came out of: "For the Kingdom of God is not a matter of what we eat or drink, but of living a life of goodness and peace and joy in the Holy Spirit . . . So then, let us therefore aim for harmony in the church and try to build each other up" (Rom 14:17, 19 NLT). Paul was writing to a church where the difference between the Jewish food rules and Gentile eating habits was creating disharmony in the church. In the same way, we can allow ethnic differences to blur our understanding of our common humanity and destroy the harmony and unity of the church. There are those who claim that, within the church in Africa, "the blood of ethnicity is thicker than the water of baptism. Those who hold this view point at Rwanda, Burundi, and Zaire, where ethnic allegiance has subordinated the bonds of the blood of Christ."[1] There Christians have murdered Christians simply because of their ethnicity, and have sometimes

---

1. Kukah, *The Church and the Politics of Social Responsibility*, 41.

been encouraged to do this by church leaders! Some massacres have even taken place within church buildings!

However, we needn't point a finger elsewhere! In my own country of Nigeria, where the majority dominates every aspect of the life of a nation, I have seen how the thirst for political and economic power has led to the demonization of my fellow human beings, in spite of their Christian faith. I am sure you could find similar situations in your own context – although you may need to pray for God to open your eyes to see them. Across the globe, humankind's search for power has distorted our understanding of the oneness of the people of God. Christians who are from majority ethnic groups still tend to see their brothers and sisters who are from minority ethnic groups as the politicians see them. This social, political, and economic reality confirms Kukah's assertion that "every Christian community bears the stamp of the human environment around which our faith is expressed."[2]

Yet Jesus's new covenant signals that a paradigm shift is necessary. And this shift is as dramatic as the one between colonialism and democracy. "God had planned something better for us" (Heb 11:40). This new covenant provides salvation for all, irrespective of the traditional world view that divides society into superior and inferior groupings (Gal 3:28). Jesus Christ provides all of us, whether we are from ethnic majorities or ethnic minorities, with access to the power of the Holy Spirit (Heb 2:4). We are a new community and must not follow the old rules dictated by tradition. We have been set free from them. But we need to allow God's changes to sweep through us.

Therefore when we elect our leaders in the church, we should not allow the considerations by which secular society is governed to dictate our actions. We should not simply appoint people from the majority group to our boards or as deacons or pastors. Instead we should adopt the attitude of the early disciples when they were considering who they should appoint to replace Judas as a witness to the resurrection. After they had made their nominations, we are told they prayed the following prayer: "Lord, you know everyone's heart. Show us which of these two you have chosen" (Acts 1:23–24). Likewise when they were choosing those who would "wait on the tables" the members of the young church were instructed to choose those "who are known to be full of the Spirit and wisdom" (Acts 6:3). The key attribute in both cases is that those chosen must be close to the Lord. The group to which they belonged was irrelevant. Do we pray like this and vote as God's Spirit reveals it to us? What happens in our churches?

---

2. Kukah, 36.

But the church in Africa does not only need to repent of showing undue deference to the majority groups internally. There are broader issues too. The smugness of the majority has meant that the African church has largely remained silent in the face of overwhelming human rights abuses suffered by minorities and by socially disrespected groups such as women, widows, children, orphans, the poor and the weak. In spite of its celebrated numerical growth, the African church has no political ideology that enables it to join the debate on social injustices on the continent. Elsewhere evangelical Protestants have at various stages in their history confronted and championed these issues. Now Africans need to face them here in Africa. Sadly however, instead of doing so, the African church often simply allies itself with the wealthy and the powerful. This is why Kamaara writes, "While Christian values are expected to foster national cohesion and identity, more often than not Christianity has provided a convenient rallying point around which ethnic conflicts are mobilised."[3]

Are we as Christians helping to create a fair society in which justice is accessible to all? Is God calling our faith community to play a role here, even if it is only to reach out to those whose need we know because it is evident in the area near our local church? Maybe God is calling us to speak out nationally and internationally against abuses that deny others their rights as God's created beings? The majority ethnic group is usually ideally situated to make a difference in local and national government. I cannot tell where this meditation will lead you.

Jesus warned the Pharisees against valuing the "most important seats in the synagogues and respectful greetings in the marketplace" more than a true knowledge of God's heart (Luke 11:43). Some of the high status people who heard him say this were upset by these words and accused Jesus of insulting them. Jesus did not back down in deference to the elite. He continued to denounce their self-satisfaction, pointing out that they were setting rules that made life difficult for the poor and were doing nothing to help the poor carry these burdens (Luke 11:46).

What will Jesus say to us when the great day comes and we bow before his judgement seat? Will he accuse us of having clung to power and status while ignoring the needs of others? Let us prayerfully consider whether we are indeed following his way or merely living in the traditions of our past.

---

3. Eunice Kamaara, "Towards Christian National Identity in Africa: A Historical Perspective to the Challenge of Identity to the Church in Kenya," in *Studies in World Christianity*, 16, no. 2 (July 2010): 1.

Learning to Live and Love as Members of a Minority Group

Some of you who read the last section are members of minority groups, part of the remnant that has survived. Some of you have first-hand experience of the type of discrimination I have been talking about. It is only natural to enjoy reading that those in majority ethnic groups should humble themselves and repent and reach out to you. It is human to feel that it is time some of this was said. But we cannot act in merely human ways. We have to act as citizens of the kingdom of heaven and there is much for us to learn too.

Adjusting Our Hearts and Minds

Like members of majority groups, members of minority groups need to lay a strong foundation of prayer before they resort to action. The stories of Ezra and Nehemiah both prove the power of prayer. But Nehemiah's prayer before he dared to approach his master the king, began with confession (Neh 1:11). And that is where we have to begin too. Only when we have admitted our faults can we pray into the situation. The story that unfolds from Nehemiah's prayer is an amazing journey into leadership.

Remember, too, the prayer of Ezra before he and the remnant set out for Jerusalem, carrying the temple treasures that had been returned to them. Well aware of the dangers of the journey, he nonetheless felt that he could not ask the king for soldiers and horsemen to protect them (Ezra 8:22–23). Instead he took his stand on the fact that "the gracious hand of our God is on everyone who looks to him" and what amazing protection God provided against corruption and attack and theft. When the remnant reached Jerusalem, every item of treasure was accounted for (Ezra 8:34).

For God to be the covenant-redeemer to either a remnant or an oppressed ethnic minority, however, they must be willing to recognize him as their Lord and redeemer by continuing to do what is good and right in his eyes (2 Chr 14:2). God will only be the God of the remnant and the oppressed minorities of Africa if they cling to him. The God of the remnant, of the minority and the majority, and of all the created universe has one equal covenant standard and expectation for all. All must love the Lord with all their heart, all their understanding and all their strength and must love their neighbour as themselves, no matter whether these neighbours are part of the majority group or of the minority remnant, whether they are rich or poor, friends or enemies, the elite or the underdogs, the admired or the despised (Mark 12:30–31).

Adjusting Our Attitudes and Actions

Most of those who listened to our Lord were the "underdogs," the conquered, the inferior in their own land. They were constantly being told what to do by the elite Pharisees and teachers of the law, who had developed a burdensome system of laws to supplement the biblical law of Moses. They were ruled by the Herod family and were under the heel of Rome. Time and again we pick up undertones indicating that the people to whom Jesus preached were waiting for him to liberate them from the yoke of Rome.

Some of those who followed Jesus must have hoped that they would be given important roles in his new dispensation once the overlords had been deposed. Even his disciples who shared his life with him thought about this and, as they travelled, they argued about "who was the greatest" (Mark 9:34). On one occasion at least Jesus was asked to consider his future "cabinet" when James and John came with their mother to suggest that they should be assigned to important positions in Christ's kingdom (Matt 20:20–21). We read that the other disciples were angry with James and John. It seems unlikely that that they were upset because they understood more about the nature of the kingdom that the two brothers did. Probably they just resented the fact that these two had tried to wriggle their way into power before the rest of them had a chance to stake their claims! The minority saw majority status as something to be grabbed.

In response, Jesus explained that his way was different. He did not promise to upgrade them. Instead he told them that they needed to change the way they thought about power:

> You know that the rulers of the Gentiles lord it over them, and their high officials exercise authority over them. Not so with you. Instead, whoever wants to become great among you must be your servant, and whoever wants to be first must be your slave – just as the Son of Man did not come to be served, but to serve, and to give his life as a ransom for many. (Matt 10:24–28)

Jesus's whole life was lived as a member of a minority. He chose to be born in a stable rather than in a palace or a wealthy home. He was raised in a village in a region that the elite scorned. "Nazareth! Can anything good come from there?" "A prophet does not come out of Galilee" (John 1:46; 8:52). Yet his whole life was not about power but about service. One of the most dramatic examples of this must surely be the event recorded shortly before his death:

> Jesus knew that the Father had put all things under his power, and that he had come from God and was returning to God; so he got up from the meal, took off his outer clothing, and wrapped a towel round his waist. After that, he poured water into a basin and began to wash his disciples' feet . . . When he had finished washing their feet, he put on his clothes and returned to his place. "Do you understand what I have done to you?" he asked them. You call me 'Teacher' and 'Lord,' and rightly so, for this is what I am. Now that I, your Lord and Teacher, have washed your feet, you also should wash one another's feet. I have set an example that you should do as I have done for you." (John 13:3–15)

Yet despite Christ's example, even in churches members of majority groups tend to look down on those who are designated as belonging to a remnant or a minority group. And minority groups find ways to look down on their fellow minorities. We are blinded by our own social, political, intellectual and economic achievements and by our assessments of others, and we fail to recognize that we are not superior to others, but that like all human beings we are beset with weaknesses. Often we are not willing to serve or to submit to others.

Those of us who belong to minority groups are quick to argue that the traditional superiority of an ethnic majority over the minorities is offensive. We argue that it is unfair, unjustified and that therefore we must stand up for our rights, even if that means rebellion and violent resistance to the authorities. This is a very human reaction! However, it is not a Christian reaction. Christ did not authorize rebellion any more than he authorized domination. In the Sermon on the Mount he dealt with one of the most unfair practices allowed under Roman authority – the right of a soldier to force someone to carry his equipment or baggage for one mile. How humiliating that must have been for a Jewish man, forced to act as a servant to a representative of the hated overlords. The only good thing that could be said about that "right" was that the law did not allow the soldier to demand any further service. One mile was the maximum that could be demanded. Yet Jesus did not suggest that people refuse to help carry the baggage or put the baggage down exactly at the milepost. Instead he told them to do more than was expected (Matt 5:41).

Commenting on this passage Tom Wright says: "Turn the tables on them, advises Jesus. Don't fret and fume and plot revenge. Copy your generous God.

Go a second mile . . . there is a different way to be human."[4] He goes on to say that "the Sermon on the Mount is not just about how to behave. It is about discovering the living God in the loving, and dying, Jesus and learning to reflect that love ourselves into the world that needs it so badly."

So members of minority groups have an incredibly important role to play in addressing issues of prejudice and unfairness, but we have to reflect Christ's ways, not our desires. The biblical concept of the remnant teaches us that we do not forfeit our dignity when we suffer humiliation. The remnant of Israel survived as God's beloved people and the source of hope for the world. No domination can change that fact. Even today remnants everywhere survive only through God's power and because of his covenant love, and they still have valuable contributions to make to their nations.

The remnant at the time of the Old Testament exile was the future hope of humanity in general and of Israel in particular. And remnants in other contexts can equally be instruments of spiritual, political and economic reformation and transformation. The biblical concept of remnant provides a sharp contrast to the majority and minority ideology that thrives in so many countries. God does not ignore a remnant. And if he cares for remnants, he will undoubtedly also care for minorities. The God of steadfast love will not neglect them, and he cares when they are oppressed. The psalmist says things like "How priceless is your unfailing love, O God! People take refuge in the shadow of your wings" (Ps 36:7). The word *people* encompasses all humanity, not just God's chosen people. And if all people can take refuge in the God of Israel, then surely all ethnic minorities can do so, particularly when their needs are ignored. Our dignity may seem to be impaired, our feelings may be hurt, but we are not abandoned.

Adjusting Our Churches and Communities

We can trust God to deliver us when we walk along his route. This does not mean, however, that we must simply stand by idly waiting for God's triumph. God provided the remnant returning from Babylon with practical skills and common sense so that they could rebuild Jerusalem. He will raise up the leaders we need; he will provide the skills we need. We must make suggestions and should propose suitable members for our church councils or diaconates. But we must do this in humility to serve the church, not our ambitions or our

---

4. N. T. Wright, *Matthew for Everyone, Part 1* (London: SPCK, 2004), 52–53.

group. It must not become a campaign to exalt minorities over others but to further God's kingdom.

Similarly, we must work to secure the representation of minority groups in our community structures, not just to fight for gains for their group but to better the condition of the entire community.

God has not forgotten the minorities. He cares. The remnant are to be "a light" that leads humanity back to their Creator, to the source of life and to the one deserving their worship, adoration, and praise (Matt 5:14). This is why the concept of the remnant applies in the political and social arena and not just in the field of God–human relationships. We are "saving" those whose lives are endangered as a result of their being in the minority group.

Conclusion

It is always easier to slip back into old patterns of living than to change. But Jesus had strong words for those who claim to follow him, or even make a start at following him, and then slip back into old ways: "No one who puts a hand to the plough and looks back is fit for service in the kingdom of God" (Luke 9:62).

The good news of Jesus Christ is the fulfilment of the Old Testament covenants and the remnant is included in those blessings. This should be a source of rejoicing for both minorities and majorities. As James reminds us, "Believers in humble circumstances ought to take pride in their high position. But the rich should take pride in their humiliation" (Jas 1:9–10). Being a minority is no cause for shame; being a majority is no cause for pride. Both are equal before God, and those who are faithful to him will receive "the crown of life that the Lord has promised to those who love him" (Jas 1:12).

This should give us courage. African Christians of all ethnic groups can hope for a bright future when the Africa that God wants emerges out of the social circumstances of the present. And in the present, we can live with the assurance that a minority that trusts and clings to God is in fact the majority, for "one plus God is a majority."

May those words guide you as you seek to live out the truths presented in this book in your community.

References

Alexander, Joseph Addison. *Isaiah Translated and Explained*. Grand Rapids: Eerdmans, 1965; Repr. 1852.

Bagu, Kajit J. (John Paul). *Peace-Building, Constitutionalism and the Global South*. London: Routledge, 2020.

Brown, Brené. *Daring Greatly: How the Courage to Be Vulnerable Transforms the Way We Live, Love, Parent and Lead*. New York: Gotham, 2012.

Friedman, Ina R. "The Other Victims of the Nazis." *Social Education* 59, no. 6 (1995): 339–341.

Hasel, Gerhard F. "Remnant." In *The Interpreter's Dictionary of the Bible: Supplementary Volume*, edited by Keith Grim. Nashville: Abingdon, 1984.

Kamaara, Eunice. "Towards Christian National Identity in Africa: A Historical Perspective to the Challenge of Identity to the Church in Kenya." *Studies in World Christianity* 16, no. 2 (2010): 126–44.

Katanacho, Yohanna, *Praying Through the Psalms*. Carlisle, UK: Langham Global Library, 2018.

Kitwood, T. M. *What Is Human?* Leicester: Inter-Varsity Press, 1970.

Kukah, Hassan Matthew. *The Church and the Politics of Social Responsibility*. Ikate-Surulere, Lagos: Sovereign Prints Nigeria, 2010.

Kunhiyop, Samuel W. *Witchcraft Belief and Accusations: A Biblical and Christian Perspective*. Jos, Nigeria: Challenge Press, 2019.

Piper, John. "God's Covenant with David." In *Desiring God: Meditation of a Christian Hedonist*, revised edition, 18 January 2014. Accessed on 12 November 2018. www.desiringgood.org/ . . . /gods-covenant-with-david.html.

Sproul, R. C., ed. *Reformation Study Bible, ESV*. Orlando, FL: Ligonier Press, 2015.

Stassen, Glen H., and David P. Gushee. *Kingdom Ethics: Following Jesus in Contemporary Contexts*. Downers Grove, IL: InterVarsity Press, 2003.

Williamson, Paul R. "Covenant." In *Dictionary of the Old Testament: Pentateuch*, edited by T. Desmond Alexander and David W. Baker. Downers Grove, IL: InterVarsity Press, 2003.

Wright, Christopher J. H. *Knowing God – The Trilogy: Knowing Jesus, God the Father, and the Holy Spirit through the Old Testament*. Carlisle, UK: Langham Global Library, 2017.

Young, E. J. *An Introduction to the Old Testament*. Grand Rapids, MI: Eerdmans, 1984.

Further Reading

Agang, Sunday Bobai. *When Evil Strikes: Faith and the Politics of Human Hostility*. African Christian Studies Series. Eugene, OR: Pickwick, 2016.

———. *No More Cheeks to Turn?* Carlisle, UK: HippoBooks, 2017.

Agang, Sunday Bobai, Dion A. Forster, H. Jurgens Hendriks. *African Public Theology*. Carlisle, UK: HippoBooks, 2020.

Bediako, Kwame. *Jesus and the Gospel in Africa: History and Experience*. Maryknoll, NY: Orbis, 2004.

Haynes, Jeff. *Third World Politics: A Concise Introduction*. Oxford: Blackwell, 1996.

Moltmann, Jürgen. *Creating a Just Future: The Politics of Peace and the Ethics of Creation in a Threatened World*. London: SCM, 1989.

Niebuhr, Reinhold. *Moral Man and Immoral Society: A Study in Ethics and Politics*. Louisville, KY: Westminster John Knox, 1932.

Rohr, Richard, and John Feister. *Jesus' Plan for a New World: The Sermon on the Mount*. Cincinnati, OH: Franciscan Media, 1996.

Stassen, Glen H. *Living The Sermon on the Mount: A Practical Hope for Grace and Deliverance*. San Francisco: Jossey-Bass, 2006.

Suchocki, Marjorie H. *The Fall to Violence: Original Sin in Relational Theology*. New York: Continuum, 1994.

CPSIA information can be obtained
at www.ICGtesting.com
Printed in the USA
LVHW081116110521
687091LV00013B/2840